EXPERIENCE THE JOY
OF DEBT-FREE LIVING

EXPERIENCE THE JOY OF DEBT-FREE LIVING

David C. Friend

EXPERIENCE THE JOY OF DEBT-FREE LIVING

Cover Designer: Kästle Olson
Interior Design and Formatting: Deborah J Ledford

Print Format ISBN: 978-1092870795

DEDICATION

This book is lovingly dedicated to my Grandmother
Bessie Matheny
1901-1971

FORWARD

"David Friend is uniquely qualified to address the sensitive issue of financial management from a personal and family perspective in a way which most pastors are not. Through practical life experience as a banker and real estate developer for twenty-eight years before entering the pastorate, David brings a wealth of knowledge to the table in discussion of scriptural principles.

For many years, David and his wife Sharon taught the largest Sunday School class at Phoenix First (and many felt in America), and in that role helped countless numbers of families get out of debt, increase their personal net worth, plan for the future of their families, give more to the work of the Lord, and prosper through godly stewardship methods.

Today, David continues to provide the financial and spiritual counsel that blesses multitudes. Now, through this book, you can benefit from this tremendous resource to the body of Christ, but don't just read this book. Study it, pour over it, and most importantly, begin to take the steps to apply these principles in your life so that you and yours, and the kingdom of God, will benefit from your obedience to God's plan for your financial well-being.

After all, remember it is the Lord who gives you the power to create wealth to establish the covenant of His kingdom on this earth.

As you benefit from these principles, you'll want to help others realize the many benefits of debt-free living and will recommend these great truths contained in this book to others."

~ Tommy Barnett, Co-Founder Dream Center Church

PREFACE

For many years, people have asked me to write a book or a training manual about setting up a simplified plan for personal finances and living debt-free. The question in my mind was, "Why do we need another book about personal finances?"

There are many well-written published books about how to handle our finances. However, so many of these books use ledgers, charts, computer software, daily postings and so forth. After working with thousands of individuals, I have discovered that the vast majority of people will not post ledgers, fill in charts, or list every dollar they spend for two or three days much less for ninety days or more.

Because of that I offer you a simplified plan you can use to organize your finances and live debt-free. For more than forty years, my wife and I have used a single piece of paper to list our expenses and keep track of our account balances. I will explain this practical exercise in detail later.

If you truly desire to be debt-free in your finances, I believe in the pages of this book you will find a realistic and sensible plan. However, let us never forget, living debt-free is a spiritual issue. May I suggest you pray for the Lord's help before reading these chapters. Ask the Holy Spirit to reveal to you what you need to do to be set free from the bondage of debt. Every type of freedom we desire in our life requires a spiritual commitment. These chapters will challenge you to look at your finances from a spiritual and common sense perspective.

It is essential to understand that expense control is far more important than finding ways to make more money. From interviewing thousands of individuals, I have come to realize that unless we work on our spending habits, additional income is only a temporary fix. I will discuss this issue in detail in later chapters. Let's look at what our primary goals are to experience debt-free living.

- Learn how to be in control of our financial decisions.

- Set up a financial plan based on the Word of God.

- Decide to get out of debt.

Start right now to claim God's promises for debt-free living. Believe you can reach this goal. Believe it will become a reality in your life. Try to imagine a plan allowing you to start with what you have today to become debt-free, including your home mortgage. In less than ten years you can be debt-free. I want to help you accomplish these goals. Before reading any further, stop and ask the Lord to help you achieve your financial goals. Pray this prayer:

"Heavenly Father, I need your touch, your direction, and your wisdom. I desire to become debt-free and experience debt-free living in my life. I submit my will to you. Speak to me as I read these pages. Thank you for your help in this area of my life. In Jesus' name I pray. Amen."

~ David C. Friend

TABLE OF CONTENTS

THE WISDOM OF PROVERBS

BEFORE WE MOVE into the body of this book on debt-free living, we must read our instructional manual found in the The New Living Translation of the word of God.

Please do not rush through these scriptures. In Proverbs 3 you will see how our God provides wisdom for making decisions in our life. May I suggest you underline the verses that provide instructions for your specific area of need?

Proverbs Chapter 3

Verse 1: *My child, never forget the things I have taught you.*
Store my commands in your heart.

Verse 2: *If you do this, you will have many years, and your life will be satisfying.*

Verse 3: *Never let loyalty and kindness leave you!*
Tie them around your neck as a reminder. Write them deep within your heart.

Verse 4: *Then you will find favor with both God and people, and you will earn a good reputation.*

Verse 5: *Trust in the Lord with all your heart; do not depend on your own understanding.*

Verse 6: *Seek his will in all you do, and he will show you which plan to take.*

Verse 7: *Don't be impressed with your own wisdom. Instead, fear the Lord and turn away from evil.*

Verse 9: *Honor the Lord with your wealth and with the best part of everything you produce.*

Verse 10: *Then he will fill your barns with grain, and your vats will overflow with good wine.*

Verse 11: *My child, don't reject the Lord's discipline, and don't be upset when he corrects you.*

Verse 12: *For the Lord corrects those he loves, just as a father corrects a child in whom he delights.*

Verse 13: *Joyful is the person who finds wisdom, the one who gains understanding.*

Verse 14: *For wisdom is more profitable than silver, and her wages are better than gold.*

Verse 15: *Wisdom is more precious than rubies, nothing you desire can compare with her.*

Verse 18: *Wisdom is a tree of life to those who embrace her; happy are those who hold her tightly.*

Verse 19: *By wisdom the Lord founded the earth; by understanding he created the heavens.*

Verse 20: *By his knowledge the deep fountains of the earth burst forth, and the dew settles beneath the night sky.*

Verse 21: *My child, don't lose sight of common sense and discernment. Hang on to them.*

Verse 22: *For they will refresh your soul. They are like jewels on a necklace.*

Verse 23: *They keep you safe on your way, and your feet will not stumble.*

Verse 24: *You can go to bed without fear; you will lie down and sleep soundly.*

Verse 25: *You need not be afraid of sudden disaster or the destruction that comes upon the wicked.*

Verse 26: *For the Lord is your security. He will keep your foot from being caught in a trap.*

Verse 27: *Do not withhold good from those who deserve it when it's in your power to help them.*

Verse 28: *If you can help your neighbor now, don't say, "Come back tomorrow, and then I'll help you."*

Verse 33: *The Lord curses the house of the wicked, but he blesses the home of the upright.*

Verse 34: *The Lord mocks the mockers but is gracious to the humble.*

Verse 35: *The wise inherit honor, but fools are put to shame.*

Gaining wisdom is crucial, in order to live a life free from debt. Throughout some of the chapters in this book you will see references to Proverbs Chapter 3. If we apply the wisdom taught in Proverbs 3 to our financial decisions we will experience freedom from debt.

May everyone experience the freedom from debt they have always dreamed about, and the freedom to trust God with their finances.

A faithful man will abound with blessings, but he who hastens to be rich will not go unpunished.
~ Proverbs 28:20 (NKJV)

CHAPTER 1

Focus on the Spare

WHEN I WAS six years old, my dad decided to introduce the game of bowling to me. For more than twenty years, I went bowling with him. The bowling was fun, but being with dad was awesome.

During the years we bowled together, my father would constantly remind me to pay special attention to picking up the spares. I would get frustrated in not getting as many strikes as I believed I deserved. Dad could see my frustration and would say these four words: "Focus on the spare." He knew if I became an excellent spare maker, someday I could become an outstanding bowler.

Sometimes after picking up a spare, I would walk back to my seat feeling somewhat happy about making the "little" spare, yet still anxious about wanting the big hit—the greatest experience a bowler can accomplish—"THE STRIKE." Dad could see my attitude, so he would lean over not to let others hear and say,

"David, if you focus on the spare, you will still post a good solid game. Besides, the strikes will take care of themselves."

February 2001, my dad went to spend eternity with his Lord and Savior Jesus Christ. The days of bowling with him have long since passed. However, the memories of loading up our bowling balls and driving to that noisy old bowling alley bring memories of joy, excitement, and just plain fun with the greatest man I ever knew.

Little did I know as a teenager, my father was teaching me a Biblical principle from which to pattern my financial decisions. This principle is found in the Book of Proverbs, Chapter 28: 20 (NKJV): *A faithful man will abound with blessings, but he who hastens to be rich will not go unpunished.*

The word faithful applies to one who is steady, consistent, and focused. In handling our finances, we must be educated in making good decisions, remain consistent with the right choices and focus on what God would have us do.

Let me suggest before you continue reading this book, to go to your Bible. Take a highlighter and mark every scripture in the Book of Proverbs that refers to money, borrowing, spending, and materialism. As you mark these verses, you will see steady, consistent instructions on how to take care of the small things (the spares). Then you will obtain a greater financial blessing of debt-free living (aka the strike).

In bowling, I knew if I was focused and faithful in making my spares, I could still bowl a pretty good game. Regarding my finances, I've discovered if I am faithful with little, I will be rewarded with much. You see, in bowling, if you miss a spare, a little thing, you need to make two consistent strikes to make up for that little mistake. The more spares you miss, the more difficult it is to recover.

In our financial decisions, the longer we avoid using a budget, the longer we make impulsive spending decisions, the harder it is to recover. The little mistakes add up and keep us from achieving a debt-free life.

As a bowler, my goal for every game was to bowl a perfect 300. Twelve consecutive strikes. Even after my opportunity to bowl a perfect game was gone by not striking in the first frame, I still had to be faithful in the remaining nine frames. Each new frame gave me a new opportunity to get a strike.

In our financial life, we should approach every opportunity as our chance to obtain a perfect financial goal. Yet, if you miss the strike, the big financial opportunity, you must still be faithful to make your spares by paying your bills on time, paying your tithes, and saving money for your future. Proverbs 28:20 (NKJV) starts with a condition for success. That condition is faithfulness. The verse ends with a warning that unfaithfulness will lead to punishment. Proverbs 28:20 reads: *A faithful man will abound with blessings, but he who hastens to be rich will not go unpunished.*

Focus on the spares in our finances.

Did I ever get my 300? I wish I could say I did, but no, I have yet to achieve this accomplishment. However, I lost count many years ago of the number of times I made eight, nine, ten or eleven strikes out of a possible twelve. Dad, I guess you are still right. Focus on the spare, and the strikes will take care of themselves.

In bowling I needed to be set free from focusing only on the strikes. In my finances I needed to be set free from focusing only on the big financial strikes and learn to be content to make the financial spares. The spares, such as budgeting and controlling spending, will bring the strike of debt-free living.

Freedom. Such a wonderful word. We live in a country where we have the freedom to do almost anything we desire. We enjoy freedom of worship, freedom of speech, and freedom to choose the work and education we desire. Yet, many have never experienced freedom from financial debt.

When I hear the word freedom, I am often reminded of the classic paintings known as "The Four Freedoms." These works of art were painted by the great American artist, Norman Rockwell. He is known as a man who was able to capture on canvas the lives of the people of America.

Inspired from a speech he heard during World War II by President Franklin D. Roosevelt about the four freedoms in America, Norman Rockwell painted four works of art, which are: freedom from want, freedom of worship, freedom from fear, and freedom of speech. All of these freedoms became a focal point for Americans during the World War II.

> # Freedom.
> # Such a wonderful word.

Some time ago, for me and my wife's wedding anniversary, our daughter Tricia and son-in-law Jack gave us two tickets to see a Norman Rockwell art exhibit.. During the tour, the Holy Spirit impressed upon me to present an illustrated sermon at our church on the Fourth of July weekend titled, "The Four Freedoms."

The sermon was based on the words of Jesus found in John 8:36 (NLT): *So if the Son sets you free, you are truly free.* My message explained how these words from Jesus, the son of God are the only way to experience freedom. To be free we must put our trust in the words of our savior. I explained how to be set free from fear, by trusting in the Lord with all of our heart and mind.

The Lord blessed the service, and many gave their heart to the Lord that day.

Although we live in a free country, and even though we talk about freedom, many people are slaves to their debt. Many Christians are not free in the area of money. As I mentioned before, God's word tells us those He sets free are free indeed. That scripture can apply to our finances, too.

As you read through the pages of this book, think about your freedoms. Try to imagine freedom to give, freedom to receive, freedom to make decisions, freedom from debt and freedom to prosper.

My prayer for you is: May everyone experience the freedom in money they have always dreamed about; the freedom in living debt-free and the freedom to trust God in their finances.

I believe you will see yourself living a life free from the bondage of debt. May you then be able to help others experience debt-free living.

My prayer for you is: "Lord, we need you to help us focus on the spares in our finances. If we take care of the small daily issues with money, you will help us attain the greater successes of debt-free living. We believe in the promises we have read in Proverbs chapter 3. May those promises become a reality in our life. In Jesus' name we pray. Amen."

NOTES:
List any financial issues where you are not free. i.e.,
spending, budgeting

_____

_____

_____

_____

_____

_____

_____

_____

_____

_____

_____

_____

_____

_____

_____

_____

_____

_____

_____

Money without spiritual growth may
become the destruction of our life.
There is nothing wrong with asking the
Lord to give us prosperity.

Prosperity is only an instrument to be used,
not a deity to be worshiped.
~ President Calvin Coolidge

CHAPTER 2

Financial Prosperity

THROUGHOUT THE BIBLE we read of the Lord's desire to have us prosper. In 3 John 2 (NLT) we read: *Beloved, I pray that you may prosper in all things and be in health, just as your soul prospers.*

When the Apostle John was inspired by the Holy Spirit to write these words, they were intended to address every area of our life, including our personal finances.

Let me give you a word of caution about financial prosperity. If your primary desire in reading this book is to become rich, then I suggest you reevaluate your motives, your priorities, and your desires. Almost every wealthy person I've ever known did not set out in business just to get rich. Getting wealthy is the byproduct of doing our best in the work we have chosen to pursue.

A tape or book about prosperity is attractive to almost everyone. Teaching about prosperity is fun, writing about prosperity is great and speaking to a group about financial prosperity will get people excited. However, we must be careful about who we listen to concerning financial prosperity.

If any lesson on financial success is not based on the word of God it will be built on the wrong foundation.

There are those who will tell you to give money to the church with a primary purpose of getting back money. By that I am referring to a teaching of giving to God making Him obligated to give financially to us. Some may even suggest a donation to their ministry will ensure a great financial return. Please don't misunderstand me. We can receive financial blessings from God when we give, however the Apostle Paul said, *Let nothing be done through selfish ambition.*

Allow me to talk to you about Financial Prosperity from a different point of view. As you can tell, I believe everyone can experience financial prosperity. However, I am reminded of a quote I used at the beginning of this chapter from President Calvin Coolidge: "Prosperity is only an instrument to be used, not a deity to be worshipped."

Prosperity is a promise from God. As a Banker I met so many who made prosperity their God. Their entire life was dedicated to seeking and serving prosperity. Seeking only prosperity is like being addicted to drugs. The more you get the more you want.

Let's look to God's word for an example of Godly prosperity. Genesis 39:2-3 (NKJV) reads: *The Lord was with Joseph, and he was a successful man; and he was in the house of his master the*

Egyptian. And his master saw that the Lord was with him and that the Lord made all he did to prosper in his hand.

In this passage, we see Joseph experience God's prosperity. The Lord provided success in all he did. The word prosperity, or to prosper, is found dozens of times in most bible concordances. It is vital to point out that all of the referenced scriptures on prosperity require Godly living.

Here are two examples:

1. Deuteronomy 29:9 (NKLV): *Therefore keep the words of this covenant and do them that you may prosper in all that you do.*

2. Chronicles 26:5 (NKJV): *He sought God in the days of Zechariah who had understanding in the visions of God and as long as he sought the Lord, God made him prosper.*

There are conditions to receive God's prosperity. The Word of God warns us of the danger of financial prosperity without righteousness. Proverbs 12:28 (NKJV) tells us: *He who trusts in his riches will fail, but the righteous will flourish like foliage.*

Many Christians have prospered financially with new homes, cars, and vacation homes. In some cases these families have fallen apart and divorce has destroyed their lives. I believe this happens when a Christian is not spiritually prepared to handle financial success.

For some, a new boat or second home in the mountains could be devastating to their walk with the Lord. Try to imagine how God must feel about blessing one of His children and then the child uses the blessing to spend every Sunday out of church.

Consider this true story of how financial prosperity without spiritual prosperity changed a life.

When I was a banker, I met a young man in his middle twenties. He was an average working guy with an average income and lifestyle. He was a pleasant person, always dressed clean, and looked very healthy and excited about life. One day he came to me and told me one of his relatives had died and left him $50,000,000 in a trust. That's right, $50 million!

This young man did not know what to do or how to invest his newfound wealth. At first, he decided to take $50,000 a month from his inheritance to live on. With the money he could afford a luxury car, beautiful home and numerous materialistic things. After only a few months, he became angry at what he called a "pitiful amount of money to live on" and hired an attorney to get more from his trust. Very soon his appearance and attitude changed drastically. He would arrive at the bank drunk or high on drugs. After a year or so, he stopped coming into the bank. Eventually, he overdosed on drugs and went on to eternity.

Money without spiritual growth became the destruction of his life. This young man was financially prosperous, yet spiritually bankrupt.

The Word of God provides many references to the danger of wealth harming our Christian walk. I believe those whom the Lord blesses with money must work even harder to maintain a strong Christian witness. They must understand that financial prosperity go hand in hand with spiritual growth.

King David gave us great instructions on how to keep prosperity and spiritual grow in balance. He was growing old as he wrote these words found in Psalm 37:4 (NKJV): *Delight yourself also in the Lord and He shall give you the desires of your heart.* Some might read this scripture as: Delight yourself in your desires.

> ## Financial gain without spiritual growth
> ## is not a blessing.

Let's look at verses 5 and 6: *Commit your way to the Lord, trust also in Him, and He shall bring it to pass. He shall bring forth your righteousness as the light, and your justice as the noonday.*

There are several keys to understanding this scripture. Let me try to break them down to reveal God's conditions for Financial Prosperity.

1. Commit your way to the Lord. Commit means to take a stand, to stick with it, not to waiver.

2. Trust in God not in more money.

3. Wait for God to bring it to pass. Patience is key to receiving anything from the Lord. Wait may mean no or not now. Yet, wait means exactly that—wait on the Lord for His guidance. Stop trying to manipulate God's Word. Waiting requires patience and trusting God.

4. Live a Godly life, evident to everyone.

5. Don't forget verse 4: *Delight yourself in the Lord.*

Another key to God blessing us with financial prosperity is found in Luke 16:10-12 (NIV): *Whoever can be trusted with very little can be trusted with much, and whoever is dishonest with very little will also be dishonest with much. So, if you have not been trustworthy in handling worldly wealth, who will trust you with true riches? And, if you have not been trustworthy with someone else's property, who will give you property of your own?*

In the above verse we can see that righteousness and blessing go hand in hand. Faithfulness and trust are inseparable. Being faithful with the little we may have today is key to whether the Lord can trust us with true riches later.

As a Pastor, many have said to me they will give financially to the church when their income increases. If you are one of those who are thinking that way, please reconsider. I call that type of giving, contingent giving. It is like telling the Lord we will give only when He gives to us first. I believe we must give from what we have now and not from what we may get someday. We must trust the Lord to provide.

There are numerous erroneous teachings on prosperity. I've heard some say we are to give only to those who have, because giving to the needy is kind of a bad investment. The Apostles Peter and Paul would never agree with that type of advice. We would most certainly see some righteous indignation from them today as a result of this type of teaching.

Another scripture pertinent to this lesson is found in James 4:2 (NKJV): *Yet you do not have because you do not ask. You ask and you do not receive because you ask this amiss, that you may spend it on your pleasures.*

There is nothing wrong with asking the Lord to prosper us. There is also nothing wrong with having wonderful possessions, luxuries, and wealth. However, let us not lose track of what our motives are for wealth, and why the Lord blesses us with abundance.

In the prosperity message, we often hear: give to get or give money to get more money back. Take a moment and think about why you give?

Following are some of the reasons people have presented to me. They are in no particular order. Some I personally agree with, others I do not.

1. I enjoy giving.

2. God's Word tells me to give.

3. God is blessing me so I can bless others.

4. I get a tax deduction.

5. So the Lord will bless me financially.

6. Because someone said give $100 and get back $10,000.

7. I feel guilty if I don't give.

8. To make a seed faith offering.

9. To see my church grow.

10. I want to give more so I get more.

11. It is God's will that I give.

12. All the authors of books about Christian finances say to give.

13. I don't know why.

14. Because the needy must have help.

15. My accountant said financially it is smart to give.

Now we should look at why the Lord wants us to give. Let me give you what I believe are the primary reasons given in God's Word:

• Because His Word directs us to give.

• Because He wants to bless us. *Give and it shall be given unto you.* (Luke 6:38 NKJV)

• Because He wants us to help others less fortunate.

Many think financial success and debt-free living are for only the lucky. They relate success to winning the lottery. Recently, I heard a TV news anchor report that more than forty percent of Americans said they expected to win the lottery in order to meet their retirement needs. If we are not careful, we may interpret the prosperity message as just being lucky. However, Christians are never lucky. They are blessed.

I do not believe in the lottery as a way to expect prosperity. However, we must never limit our God in the ways He may want us to prosper. The book of Isaiah, 55:8 tells us that His ways are higher than our ways.

Expecting to hit the lottery or get a $100,000 check in the mail from giving to some evangelist is an unrealistic plan to prosper financially. By trusting in God and following His wisdom found throughout the Book of Proverbs, we will be successful with our finances. We will undoubtedly prosper and even achieve a debt-free life.

Because so many play the lottery, I need to give you my thoughts. You might be surprised to find out how often members of our church have asked me to pray over their lottery ticket. They tell me if they win, the church will get some of it. As you can probably guess, I do not pray over any form of gambling. Serving God is not a gamble, it is a sure thing.

A man asked me once, "Why do only the unsaved win the lottery?" He went on to say, "If God would allow me to win, I would give greatly to His work." Yet, when I asked him if he was a tither and gave 10% of his income, he became irritated and walked away.

Let's look at the lottery and followers of Jesus Christ. Now I realize most Christians believe there is nothing wrong in buying lottery tickets. Personally, I don't believe Christians should buy them. I believe my thoughts are supported in the Word of God. We would be better off putting that $1 in the offering basket. We could give a seed faith offering of $1 and trust the Lord to bless us instead of buying a $1 lottery ticket.

Our confidence and trust must be totally given to God in order to get His attention and receive His blessing in our finances. The purchasing of a lottery ticket may be the first step in creating a hope in gambling to meet our financial needs. If you would have spent the amount of time I have trying to help those with a gambling addiction, you might better understand my reasoning.

Previously I said that I wanted to approach prosperity from a different perspective. Stay with me on this thought. We have all heard the saying, "You can't take it with you." The comment, "I've never seen a U-Haul following a hearse," is often told as a joke. Yet, I would like to challenge the first comment and say the Word of God shows us a way, in a spiritual sense, that we can take our prosperity with us. Let me explain my reasoning.

Jesus said in Matthew 6:19-21 (NKJV): *Do not lay up for yourselves treasure on earth, where moth and rust destroy and where thieves break in and steal; but lay up for yourselves treasures in heaven, where neither moth nor rust destroys and where thieves do not break in and steal. For where your treasure is, there your heart will be also.*

Every time we decide to spend, invest, or give money, we are deciding what is most important to us. I believe the Lord is not opposed to us having possessions and financial security. However, in addition to spending our money on our needs, wants, and desires; we must also give to others in need.

When we invest our money in paying tithes or giving offerings, we are investing our substance in eternity. When we give to help an inner city outreach lead people to Jesus, our money is invested in eternity. Therefore, when we achieve our reward of eternal life with our Lord and Savior Jesus Christ, I believe we will see our investments in heaven in hundreds or even thousands of souls spending eternity with us. This is what I am referring to when I say we can take it with us.

I realize many of you want to give to the work of the Lord but you can't see a way to do it. In Chapters 2, 5, and 10, you will find the way to start giving and start laying up treasure in heaven.

My prayer for you is: "Lord, our prayer is we will never become a slave to obtaining financial prosperity. We can experience debt-free living and have freedom in our finances when we learn to trust our God and keep our motives pure. Spiritual prosperity must always precede financial prosperity. Help us Lord to seek first the things you desire. When we do that we will establish a foundation on which you will be able to build. We will live our life free from debt if we follow your directions. May we trust you in every area of our life. Thank you Lord for your desire to help us be debt-free. In Jesus' name we pray. Amen."

NOTES:
How do you plan to prosper?

_____

_____

_____

_____

_____

_____

_____

_____

_____

_____

_____

_____

_____

_____

_____

_____

_____

_____

_____

As Christians we know we must sow
in order to reap.

Before giving offerings, pray and ask the Holy Spirit to help us decide how much to give and to whom we should give.

You cannot serve God and riches.
~ Matthew 6:24 (NKJV)

CHAPTER 3

Tithing and Debt-Free Living

HAVE YOU EVER wondered why some churches have stopped talking about tithing? Why do so many pastors feel uncomfortable in asking their congregations to give money to the church? As a pastor for over twenty years I have seen many churches stop passing the offering plate during the service. We see offering stations placed in the lobby instead of the traditional way of taking up offerings in church. In my opinion, we are robbing our congregations from receiving the joy of giving as they come together in a church service. This chapter is dedicated to clarifying how giving and tithing leads to debt-free living.

Authors have written hundreds, maybe thousands of books on tithing. Some teach, "Give dollars to get dollars." Some say, "Give money and don't expect anything." Others believe tithing is an Old Testament teaching and does not apply to New

Testament teaching.

First we need to understand why we give. Then we need to see how we will be able to give. That is when we can become free to tithe. As Christians, we know we must sow in order to reap. We have all heard that it is more blessed to give than to receive. We know God loves a cheerful giver. That is found in 2 Cor. 9:7 (NKJV). When it comes to tithing, I like what Colossians 3:23-24 (NKJV) says: *And whatever you do, do it heartily, as to the Lord and not to men, knowing that from the Lord you will receive the reward of the inheritance; for you serve the Lord Christ.*

I believe we must tithe because we love God. We must tithe in obedience to God, not merely because of emotions or need.

Joshua 1:8 (NKJV) reads: *This Book of the Law shall not depart from your mouth, but you shall meditate in it day and night, that you may observe to do according to all that is written in it. For then you will make your way prosperous, and then you will have good success.*

Mal. 3:10 (NKJV) says: *Bring all the tithes into the storehouse.* I believe tithing increases our faith in God. Tithing is not a condition to salvation, but it is a condition to establish trust in the Lord for your finances. As a matter of fact, I don't believe we deserve to ask the Lord for prosperity, debt-free living or financial abundance unless we are tithing. That statement may run some of you off, yet those who truly want to live debt-free and experience financial freedom will stay with me.

In more than forty years of helping Christians with their

finances, I have never had a single person tell me they wish they had never tithed. Yet thousands have desired to become tithers or wanted to get back to tithing.

In the following chapters, I will show you how to start tithing. Many Christians become frustrated because they want to tithe, but no one has ever taken the time to show them how. Deciding to tithe is a choice. Why a Christian would not want to give at least 10% of their income to the work of the Lord is a little hard for me to understand.

People have so many excuses why they do not believe in tithing or why they can't afford to tithe. If you desire to live debt-free, why not try tithing? What do you have to lose? Maybe, just maybe, our God would be pleased if you decided to trust Him and give of your finances to His work. Proverbs 3:5 (NKJV) says: *Trust the Lord with all your heart and lean not on your own understanding.* The Lord does not want to break us financially. He does not want to put us in the poor house. However, God's Word is filled with examples and instructions on how we must give in order to receive.

We must take a step of faith when tithing in our finances. From this day forward, some need to ask the Holy Spirit to reveal to them how they can start tithing. After reading this book you will be able to see how you will be able to tithe if that is your desire.

After we begin to give 10% of our income in tithing to our local church we can move on to the next form of giving called offerings. Giving offerings do not apply to the tithe. An offering is giving above the tithe. Offerings are a gift to a special need like missionaries, the homeless or charities we desire to help.

This might be a good time to address one of the most frequently asked questions I have received about tithing: "Should I tithe on my net or my gross income?" My answer to that question is: do we want to be blessed on our gross or net income?

In John 8:36 (NKJV) Jesus said these words: *Therefore, if the Son makes you free, you shall be free indeed.*

We all know Jesus was speaking of being free from the bondage of sin and death. However, I believe this freedom should be applied to every area of our life. To be made free means to be liberated from something. To be made free is to come from bondage or slavery. Today, so many are bonded in slavery to money. They want get it so badly or they want to keep it so much they are actually held captive by it.

The scriptural references I gave in Proverbs 3 at the beginning of the book applies to being free from the bondage of financial sin. Sin is anything separating us from God. Financial bondage separates us from the blessings of the Lord. Not having financial freedom is like building a wall between the Holy Spirit and us. He is standing just outside that wall wanting to break it down and free our minds and hearts from financial bondage. We will never live debt-free until we are free in every area of our financial decisions.

This may seem a little heavy to some, so let me remind you of the words Jesus gave us concerning our finances. Matthew 6:24 (NKJV) says: *No one can serve two masters; for either he will hate the one and love the other, or else he will be loyal to the one and despise the other. You cannot serve God and mammon (riches).*

Jesus wanted to help us understand serving God must always be first in the area of money. Giving of our tithes and offerings puts the Lord first.

Let me ask you a question. Why are less than ten percent of professing Christians paying tithes (according to numerous surveys)? In some churches, only five or six percent of the congregation tithe. Remember, tithing is a full 10% of your gross income. Let me give you the results of a study I did on my own. I've worked through the numbers on this study dozens of times using the attendance and denominations of various churches.

I challenge you to do the math on your church. Take the total number of giving units you have that attend and give to your church. A giving unit is defined as every separate family. A person who is single is a giving unit. Some giving units may be a married couple. Another unit may be a family of three or more. For this study, determine how many individual giving units attend your church.

Now, go to your nearest university and obtain the demographics of your city or area. They will provide you educational make-up information-the, number of persons in each home, the age of the population, the gross medium income per household, and gross medium income per head of household. Use the medium gross income per household. In my area, it's about $100,000 per household. Now take 10% of gross income ($100,000) and you get $10,000 per household. Multiply that number by the number of giving units that give to your church. You will come up with what the income of your church should be if everyone tithed 10% of their income.

A church with 100 giving units where all tithe and have a medium income of $50,000 should have a $500,000 annual income.

As a banker I received requests from churches to refinance their mortgages or provide a line of credit for operating expenses. When I reviewed the income of a church I had to evaluate how much their income would be based on the size of their membership. My investigation of church income revealed some interesting things about giving. Most of the churches I worked with would receive about $1000 a year, per member.

A church of 100 including children had an income of $100,000 a year. That was consistent regardless of the size of the church membership. My research revealed that only five percent to eighteen percent of a church's giving units are tithing. Wow, that says a lot about how many Christians are free to tithe and how many are not.

If you want to tithe but have not known how to do it, then you will enjoy Chapter Ten in this book.

This information was not written to condemn anyone.

Yet you must agree it's a fascinating way to look at the issue of tithing.

As I have mentioned previously, the word of God addresses money, concerning the improper and proper use of it more than it speaks on Love. You may find this hard to believe, but it's true. The Lord knew we would struggle with money. He warns us about the love of money and how it will cause us to fall into sin. Friendships and family relationships have been destroyed because of the challenges of the improper use of money. Today money is the number one problem in marriage. It is also the number one reason given for divorce.

What can we do? How can we be set free from the bondage of debt? How can we put an end to money ending relationships?

Well, I am so glad you asked. It is so easy when we put our trust in God's word. First, we must surrender control of our finances to the Lord. We do it by tithing on our income.

Next we look into His word for direction. Again I recommend Proverbs Chapter 3. Throughout the Book of Proverbs we find help with our financial decisions.

My purpose is that everyone who reads these words will see how our God has developed a plan to prosper his people. He wants us to be debt-free.

My prayer for you is: "Heavenly Father help those who desire to become debt-free understand how giving of their tithes to your church will help them become a better steward of your provision. May every one of us put you first in our finances. I thank you Lord for the desire in the hearts of your followers to become financially free. May this concept of spiritual financial instruction become a reality in their lives. Some things are taught and some are caught. This teaching must be caught in order to cause a change in the desire to become debt-free. Bless everyone who reads these words. In Jesus' name I pray. Amen."

Therefore, if the Son makes you free, you shall be free indeed.

~ John 8:36 (NKJV)

NOTES:
What is keeping you from tithing?

_____

_____

_____

_____

_____

_____

_____

_____

_____

_____

_____

_____

_____

_____

_____

_____

_____

_____

_____

_____

God is our source, and discipline is the key
to allowing Him to bless us.

*In all your ways acknowledge Him and He
shall direct your path.*
~ Proverbs 3:6 (NKJV)

CHAPTER 4

Goals Set Us Free

WHENEVER I THINK about goals, I am reminded of a single mom I once counseled in the area of her finances. Let's give her the name Karen. She made an appointment to see me about how she could complete her education, get a good job, buy a home, and provide for her two young children. At first, the situation seemed very bleak. However, I could see that Karen had set some very aggressive goals and I wanted to help her develop a plan to achieve them.

We met a couple of times to determine what she needed to do in order to accomplish these goals. Karen believed the Lord would provide. She put her trust in God's word. Proverbs 3:5 (NKJV) was a constant help to her: *Trust in the Lord with all your heart and lean not on your own understanding.*

Verse 6 reads: *In all your ways acknowledge Him and He shall direct your path.* Karen also knew it would take time but with God's help, she knew she could accomplish her goals. Prov. 28:20 (NKJV) reads: *A faithful man will abound with blessings.*

Karen never asked for a handout from anyone. During this challenging time, she was faithful to church and joined the choir. Only two years after our first meeting, Karen had completed her education, bought a new home, and had a wonderful job to help her provide for her family. Congratulations Karen! You were faithful with little, and the Lord has been faithful to you in much.

Now, some are wondering how Karen accomplished all of her goals. Let me show you. During this period of time, Karen was a faithful tither on her gross income. You see Karen did not believe her God was limited in how He could bless her. She got the attention of her Lord when she was faithful with little.

Following are some suggested steps you can take to help you obtain your goal of debt-free living:

• Pray about financial decisions. If married, pray with your spouse. If single, pray with a close Christian friend or relative.

• Begin to tithe.

• Prepare a budget (expense plan—for those who think the word budget is a dirty word). Chapter Five will help you.

• Concentrate on expenses. Focus on controlling how you

spend, see (Chapter Eight).

• Start to reduce debts, see (Chapter Six).

• Every year look at the total of the previous year's debt. Has your debt gone up or down? Discover what is causing your debt to increase or decline.

• Start saving, even if it's only $10 a month. Increase to $10 a week as soon as possible.

• See how long you can keep from using your savings account.

• Set a goal to have six months of living expenses in a savings account.

• Buy enough life insurance to provide for your family's needs. Some recommend $100,000 worth of insurance for every $10,000 of income you need.

• Decide to work towards being debt-free (see Chapter Seven).

• Live within your means—this will provide for savings and investments.

Many Christians have told me they don't believe it's proper to set goals, they believe goal setting limits God and puts your trust in the goal or plan and not in the Lord. The answer to that statement is found in Proverbs 16:9 (NKJV): *A man's heart plans his way but the Lord directs his steps.*

Today, people may set goals that are easy to accomplish. They set goals based on their ability and their understanding. Why not set some goals that are beyond your understanding and ability? When we start to set goals bigger than us, we will learn to depend on the Lord to help us achieve those goals. The bigger the goal the bigger our need for the Lord.

The difficulty in reaching big goals is in submitting to the Lord and letting Him direct our steps. The Lord directs our steps when we pray daily, read His word, and get godly counsel. Goal setting and planning requires an honest effort on our part. Just like the single mom, Karen, who wanted to complete her education, get a good job, buy a home, and provide for her children; you will achieve your goal of debt-free living and financial freedom when you plan and let the Lord direct your steps.

Before we close this chapter on goals, I want you to close your eyes and start to dream about what you will do when you are debt-free. What do you want to give to the work of the Lord when you are financially able to help build the Kingdom of God? Who would you like to help? What evangelist, church or charity would you like to bless? Think of a past dream you have given up on because of being in debt. Where would you like to travel? What classes would you like to take to complete your education?

Now change your thinking and start to believe God is your source. Accept the fact that discipline is the key to allowing Him to bless us. If you have a desire to visit Israel, see yourself walking in the very places Jesus walked, praying on the Mount of Olives. Try to see yourself standing at the edge of the Sea of Galilee. Think of the experiences you could tell to your children, grandchildren, your family, friends, and work associates.

You see, dreaming and goal setting are healthy activities for all of us. My prayer for you is to dream big and set big goals, because we serve the greatest and most awesome God the world has ever known. Now look up Ephesians 3:20 (NKJV) and read about your inheritance in Christ: *Now to Him who is able to do exceedingly abundantly above all that we ask or think according to the power that works in us.*

That power is for all believers.

That power will give us the help we need to set a goal of living a debt-free life. That power will make the goal of debt-free living become reality.

My prayer for you is: "Lord, may everyone who reads these words decide to set a goal of living debt-free. The desire of your heart Lord is to bless your people. I believe your followers will believe in their hearts that you desire to help them in every area of life. May they trust in your word and follow your plan in their finances. In Jesus' name I pray. Amen."

NOTES:
List your goals.

_____

_____

_____

_____

_____

_____

_____

_____

_____

_____

_____

_____

_____

_____

_____

_____

_____

_____

_____

Decide to take the proper steps toward
freedom in your finances.

Let's not look at this chapter as a challenge,
but as an opportunity that will
lead us to living debt-free.

CHAPTER 5

Expense Plan

WHEN DISCUSSING FINANCES, I am reminded of a couple who were discussing their budget, and the wife said to her husband, "This budgeting is easy as long as you don't pay any attention to the miscellaneous."

For most people, budgeting requires change. Life is full of change. Let's try a little exercise:

Write the word BUDGET on the following line with your right hand:

_____

Now, write the word BUDGET on the next line with your left hand.

_____

If you are left handed reverse the process. Unless you have trained yourself to write with either hand, you probably had to struggle with it like I did. When I wrote the word "Budget" with my left hand, it looked like a bad sketch of a mountaintop. The purpose of this little exercise is to show you how it is easy to do something we have always done, but to try something different is difficult. To change a habit requires some work. To change bad habits, takes even more work.

Discussing the word "Budget" is a challenge for any author writing a book about finances. The word "Budget" causes most people to get discouraged. Let's not look at this chapter as a challenge but as an opportunity leading us to debt-free living.

Obviously, preparing an expense plan (budget) is crucial to every healthy financial program. As a Pastor, I have asked my congregation the question, "How many expect the church to set a budget and to operate within that budget?" Every hand goes up instantly. Then I ask "how many of you have a budget and how many of you operate within it?" Only four or five percent raise a hand. In more than forty years of helping Christians set up biblically-based practical expense plans, I am always amazed at how many don't have any type of written budget. Yet, those same individuals would blow a fuse if their church operated without a budget.

This chapter is key to helping you know where you are today financially. It will focus on how much you are spending every month. What does it cost you to live each month based on the entire year? Please take this chapter to heart. Unless you know what it costs you to live every month, you will never be able to save, invest or live debt-free.

My experience with singles and couples reveal 95% are spending $300.00 to $1,000.00 per month more than they make. Some may wonder how they can spend more than they make. Usually the culprits are credit card debt increases or savings decrease. Sometimes a loan consolidation will hide poor spending habits.

On one occasion, I was helping a young couple look at their expenses. After listing every expense, we discovered they were spending over $800.00 per month more than they earned. They could not believe this was possible. However, their debt had increased $50,000 during the last five years. This young couple was refinancing their home every year and that made them feel they were "paying off" debt. Fortunately, the value of their home had increased $50,000 during the same time frame. This refinancing disguised a pattern of overspending. Just imagine every year going $10,000 deeper in debt and not being aware of it. Seems a little impossible, yet I frequently meet couples with similar stories.

The only way to keep your finances off this road to financial failure is to know how much it costs you and your family each month to live. I want to challenge you! Most people will not take the fifteen-twenty minutes it takes to list their expenses each month. Most will keep on blaming something or someone for their spending. They will complain about not having enough income.

Take some time to list your expenses. The following page provides a tool you can use to take your step of action toward living debt-free.

Don't forget to plan for non-monthly expenses, for example clothing, car repairs, vacations etc. These items are noted with an asterisk.

Let me give you a little help to monitor your spending. I have prepared two simple charts to help you organize your spending and income. In column (A) fill in what you believe is the correct amount you spend each month. After completing column (A), monitor what you actually spend for thirty days in each category. Enter the actual amount spent in column (B).

EXPENSES	(A) ESTIMATED AMOUNT	(B) ACTUAL AMOUNT
Tithe		
Housing Payment		
Home - Maintenance		
Car Gas		
Car Payment		
Food & Misc.		
Telephone		
Water/Trash		
Electricity		
Gas for Home		
Car Insurance		
Recreation/Meals Out		
Life/Health Insurance		
*Clothing		
Children's School		
*Medical/Dental Ins or Costs		
Savings		
*Gifts -Christmas, Birthdays, etc.		
Misc: Dry Cleaning, Haircuts,		
Loan Payment		
TOTAL		

*Denotes Non-Monthly expenses.
Delete or add specific items in your budget.

EXPENSES	Suggested % - Adjust to 100%
Tithe	10% of Gross Income
House Payment	30-35% of Net Income
Home Maintenance	2% of Net Income
Car Insurance	2% of Net Income
Car Payment	5% of Net Income
Electricity	4% of Net Income
Water/Trash	1% of Net Income
Telephone	1% of Net Income
Gas Home	1% of Net Income
Gas Auto	1% of Net Income
Insurance Health/Life	2% of Net Income
Entertainment	5% of Net Income
Food	10% of Net Income
Kid's School Expense	2% of Net Income
Gifts	3% of Net Income
Dry Cleaning, Haircuts, etc	1% of Net Income
Loan Payment/s	Varies
Clothing	2% of Net Income
Savings	10% of Net Income
Total %	

Renting vs. owning will change categories.
Percentage will vary on income percentages.

After thirty days, you will have a better understanding of what you actually spend. Don't forget to include the non-monthly expenses like gifts and vacation. This exercise will give you your actual expenses to set up your monthly budget. I realize these percentages may add up to more than 100%. You must adjust these percentages to meet your personal budget and equal 100%. This is only a guide, and your actual percentages may vary.

Use these charts to compare how your estimated expenses match up to your actual expenses. For those who are paid twice a month, list your expenses for each pay period. You will need to determine which expenses come out of each pay period.

There is a reward for those who set up a budget after determining their actual spending and income. That reward will be to live a debt-free life.

When you know what your actual expenses are each month you will be able to determine how much you are really spending. It will be either more or less than your income. For those who spend more than they make, do not jump to the conclusion you need to make more money. Although it is always nice to make more, it is usually better to learn how to spend less.

Our Government never spends less. Their spending budget increases every year. We must stop constantly increasing our spending and start to focus on how we can spend less. This will not be easy, but the rewards of it will be great.

Every time you get frustrated with this new budgeting plan try to think of how it will feel to be debt-free. I believe in you and your ability to meet this challenge oops opportunity. More importantly, I believe our God will help you accomplish your goal of debt-free living.

My prayer for you is: "Heavenly Father, many who have read this chapter may struggle with it. Help them to understand the value in preparing a budget and live within that budget. May everyone use these charts to help organize their spending. When we know how much we spend it will help us become better stewards of what you have provided for us. Help us to realize that more income may not be the only answer to becoming debt-free. Bless each individual who desires to control their spending. In Jesus' name I pray. Amen."

NOTES:
Start now to budget. Set a time and date.

Develop a new way of thinking about your finances.

The miracle in your finances is your commitment to change.

CHAPTER 6

Find the Miracle in Your Finances

MY FRIEND AND mentor, Pastor Tommy Barnett, wrote a book titled, *There's A Miracle in Your House.* In this book he tells us everything we need to build a great church is within our congregation. That is great advice for anyone who wants to see a miracle in their life.

Well, I believe there is a miracle in your finances! The miracle may be a mental change in making financial decisions. I believe the seed is there in our finances to produce our miracle. All we need to do is find the seed, water it, help it grow, and it will produce our miracle.

You could say we can grow our own plan to live a debt-free life with what we already have. As you review the steps in this chapter, use them to help you find the seed for your financial miracle.

The first step is to find ways to reduce your spending. There have been numerous books written on how to save on things like insurance, bank fees, automobile purchases, utility costs, and more.

Following is my list of the Most Common Areas to Find Money in Your Budget:

1. Avoid paying service fees for checking accounts.

2. If your bank does not provide free checks, buy your checks through a private company. They are usually less expensive. Use less checks and more debit card purchases.

3. Avoid monthly service fees on insurance premiums or on any monthly bill that charges for a monthly billing.

4. If you live in an area where utilities increase significantly during the summer or winter, you may be able to get your monthly payment set up with an averaged amount over the twelve months. In addition, teach yourself to monitor the thermostat. Adjusting the setting up or down could save you significantly on utility costs.

5. Shop for car insurance with three to five companies. Examine the need for coverage such as medical payments, towing, and so on. Seek help in this area from a competent agent.

6. Telephone bill on a land line or cell phone. I realize using land lines are declining. Long distance is a dangerous budget

killer. Negotiate a better rate with the phone company. Shop for the best rates on cell or land lines.

7. Limit the use of the ATM to withdraw cash. Once a week is often enough. Overuse of an ATM for cash will harm a budget. It shows a poor discipline pattern.

8. Pets. This is very personal, however, not everyone can afford a pet. There are expenses to consider besides food, such as routine shots and veterinarian costs.

9. Evaluate the expenses in owning a home, such as the following: insurance, utilities, hot water use, electric or gas dryer use, pest control and outside maintenance.

10. Stop newspaper or publication subscriptions and delivery. Purchase these only on the day you actually read them. Recently I canceled home delivery and signed up for the E-newspaper version at a 75% discount.

11. Shop monthly internet costs. Avoid a long term contract.

12. Cable television—Avoid purchasing more services than you really need.

13. Evaluate your life-style spending habits (treats, snacks, eating out).

14. Health club dues. Do you actually use the facility?

15. Avoid fees for a check written without sufficient funds

by getting a small credit line to back up your checking balance. Never use this as a credit line for new purchases.

16. Try not to charge anything on a credit card unless you can pay it off every month. Credit card debt is one of the most expenses forms of debt. If you pay the minimum payment it could take up to 25 years to pay off the balance.

17. Buying a new car instead of one that is at least three years old will probably do more to harm your budget than almost anything else. A new vehicle depreciates in value from the moment you drive it off the car lot. The first year it drops approximately 20%. The second year the value is reduced by 10 to 15%. Buying a good used car is almost always better than buying new. Depreciation has already hit a used automobile. My recommendation is to purchase a three-year-old vehicle. Always have the vehicle checked for mechanical performance.

18. One of the most difficult items to handle in a budget is the category known as miscellaneous. Set a fixed dollar amount on miscellaneous spending and live within it.

19. Develop a new way of thinking about your finances. Making more money is probably not the only solution to living debt-free. Choices in how you spend your money are more important than how much we make.

20. Couples: Pray together about your financial decisions.

21. Don't give up on you goal to be debt-free.

22. Understand the only thing most people lack in their financial plan is discipline.

23. Make a list of the things you buy that you do not really need. When shopping make a list and stay focused on the list.

24. Evaluate your Life Insurance costs. Work with a qualified insurance broker. Obtain several quotes before purchasing.

25. Look at the cost of Mortgage Life Insurance. Compare it to Term Insurance. Seek competent help before making this decision.

26. Reevaluate your deductibles on all of your insurance. Increasing deductibles may save on your costs. Be careful and seek council from a qualified agent.

27. Check to see if you are paying for medical coverage on your auto and home. Ask your agent if your health insurance will cover these claims.

28. Purchasing insurance from companies with the highest ratings is wise.

[Remember my comments about insurance should be discussed with a professional insurance agent. My comments are about some of the things you may want to check out. If necessary seek legal advice.]

Following are suggestions for the proper use of credit cards. Some tell you to cut up all your cards and never use them. That advice is good if you do not have the discipline to work with credit cards. I believe you have the discipline in you and all you need to do is bring forth that discipline:

29. As I said before; avoid the use of credit cards if you cannot pay them off each month.

30. Keep your credit card limits low enough to keep you from getting into serious debt, yet high enough to meet your needs.

31. Although credit cards can be a financial death sentence, proper use of a single card can be a useful tool in tracking where you are spending.

32. Obtain a credit card that provides air miles or a cash refund for every dollar you spend. By charging gas, food, and utilities monthly (and holding back the funds to pay them off monthly), you can accumulate enough miles to get a free flight or cash to purchase something you want or need.

33. Avoid any annual fee for a credit card.

34. If you are in debt to credit cards, you may want to consolidate them into one new card by using the offer many companies give to get your business. They may provide a low

transfer rate on your balances for up to a year or more. As soon as the low transfer rate offer runs out, move your balance to another institution offering a similar plan. Keep doing this until your balance is paid off. This will save you significantly in finance fees.

35. When making a purchase, ask the retailer how much of a discount you may have if you pay cash instead of using credit. The retailer is probably paying a fee to the credit card company and you may be able to get your purchase at a small discount.

36. Look carefully at the numerous credit card offers. Most people get five or more offers a month. Some of these offers provide services and discounts that will save you money.

The next few suggestions will help you find more miracles (save money) in your finances:

37. Seek professional counsel in every suggestion I have listed.

38. As you redo your budget, try to find a way to contribute to a retirement fund. An IRA, 401K, or company retirement plan are a few of the opportunities available. Seek help in selecting which retirement plan is best for you. Please do not procrastinate. A penny saved is yours, a penny spent you will probably never see again. Borrowing money to fund an IRA may be a great investment; ask your accountant if this will benefit you.

39. Sit down with a good tax accountant and find the

hundreds of opportunities (legally) you may have to pay less income taxes. Many people think they don't need an accountant or they can use a friend to get advice on their income taxes. I suggest you get to know a good, qualified, highly recommended accountant and reevaluate your tax planning. The fee you pay will probably be saved many times over from your accountant's knowledge and experience.

40. Every time you donate something to a charity, get a receipt. Whether it is cash or an item of clothing. Keep good records. Your donation to Goodwill or The Salvation Army may be deductible. You can establish a fair market value for each item and attach it to your receipt from the charity. Many people give away hundreds, even thousands of dollars, in donations annually and yet never file it in their tax returns. Always seek competent tax help with these items or call the IRS for some assistance.

Many of the people I talk to dream of starting their own business, and many of them do. However, few set up proper accounting records to properly benefit from these businesses. We owned our own business for many years and with the help of a good accountant, we have been able to save thousands of dollars in taxes. Good records, competent counsel are vital in this area.

Let's look at a few ways you can save money on your home mortgage:

41. Instead of obtaining the standard 30-year loan, try to qualify for a 10- or 15-year loan. The payment will be higher than a 30-year loan, but you will save tens of thousands of dollars in interest over the years.

42. Contact your mortgage lender to see if you can pay one-half of your payment on the 15th of the month prior to your due date on the 1st and the other 1/2 of your payment on the due date. Only about ten percent of the lenders I've contacted will allow it. If your lender will allow you to do this, you can pay off your loan several years sooner than scheduled on a 30-year loan. Pay this directly to your lender only. Do not use an agency for this, as they might charge you excessive fees.

43. Another way to reduce the length of time you will pay on a 30-year loan is to add additional principle payments to your monthly scheduled payment. Let's say you pay $1,000 per month on your home and this includes principle, interest, property taxes, and insurance. By adding $100 a month to your $1,000 payment and advising the lender that this $100 extra is to be applied toward your principle balance, you will save thousands of dollars in interest over the term of your loan.

44. Consider using VA financing if you qualify.

45. Seek help in obtaining State or Federal first-time home buyer incentives.

46. Pray for the Lord's help to get out of debt. (This should

have been #1.

You *can* and you *will be* debt-free.

Chapter Seven will cover the financial freedom you can experience by being debt-free. There is a miracle in your finances.

My prayer for you is: "Heavenly father, help those who review their daily and monthly expenses to find the sometimes hidden miracles that may reduce their cost of living. May we all look for ways to reduce our spending. Help us Lord to be sensitive to the differences between our needs, wants and desires. Reveal to us the miracles that are in our expenses. Thank you in advance for your help. In Jesus' name I pray."

NOTES:
Pick from my list of 46. What you will do and then do it!

_____

_____

_____

_____

_____

_____

_____

_____

_____

_____

_____

_____

_____

_____

_____

_____

_____

_____

_____

_____

_____

Most do not realize if they continue to make the minimum payment on their credit cards, it could take more than 25 years to pay them off.

Say this often to yourself:
"Debt-free.
I will be debt-free."

CHAPTER 7

Believe You Can Get Out Of Debt

WE MUST UNDERSTAND what is a blessing and what is a curse. One day a lady ran up to me after church. She was beaming with joy and excitement. She said the Lord had blessed her with a new car and it was a beautiful silver color SUV with a leather interior and built-in video screens. Then I heard the words, "It's an SUV that meets all my needs." That is when she told me the price was only $635 a month for seven years. As soon as I heard her make that statement, I felt a little sad for her.

I did not want to burst her bubble, but what is a need? What is a want? What is a blessing? What is a curse? I believe it takes only a little common sense to know the difference.

Do the blessings of the Lord come with a monthly price tag exceeding what we can afford? You see, before she went to buy the SUV, she felt $350 a month would fit into her budget. Do we really believe a $635-a-month payment is a blessing from God?

Do we understand the difference between a need and a want? Do we allow someone to talk us into purchasing something we can't afford? Do we ignore our budget? Had this lady evaluated these questions?

I am confident, like most of those who get into huge debt on a vehicle, she looked only at her wants and desires and not her real need. What could I say after she had already made the purchase? All I said was, It is a beautiful SUV. Let me ask you, was this a blessing or a curse?

Getting out of debt is a dream for everyone who is in bondage to debt. Take a moment now, close your eyes, and imagine being debt-free. Say it to yourself—"I am debt-free."—It has a nice sound to it. It's very peaceful and comforting, yet most Americans will never be able to say it.

Over the years I have heard many say "I'm debt-free." Then they follow up with; all I owe is my mortgage payment. Well a mortgage payment is an obligation we owe. Until it is paid off we are not really debt-free. In reality home owners are never free from paying something to someone for the privilege of owning their home. As a home owner we will always be required to pay property taxes, (depending on the state) property insurance and possibly a fee to a home owners association.

In order to be debt-free, including our home mortgage, we need to take a closer look at our monthly mortgage payment. How did our mortgage payment get to be the amount it is today? Has refinancing or a debt consolidation hidden your increase in mortgage debt?

Recently I heard a mortgage lender tell a group they should refinance their home and get cash back so they could take a vacation or buy furniture. That is some of the *worst* advice I have ever heard. We should never take our home equity to purchase something that will decline in value, or have no nominal value at all. Our home equity should be protected for our retirement. The equity in our home is usually our largest asset. Telling someone to use home equity for a vacation or buy clothes is like telling a drug addict how to find another source to get their drugs.

Using our home equity to pay off other debt is very risky. Hiding debt in a home refinance will never allow us to be debt-free. The only way to become free from debt is to find a way to decrease our debt.

Please listen carefully as you read the following two sentences. Then read them over and over until you get them into your heart.

Say out loud: "Debt is caused by my spending."

Say out loud: "How much I make may not be the solution to get out of debt?"

We would be better off if we decided to spend more time on controlling spending, and less time on worrying about how much we make or how we can make more. Every one of us could do a better job in how we spend money. As a matter of fact, we can do something about spending today. On the other hand few of us can do very much about how much we will make today.

Debt is not sin, however how we obtained that debt may be. If we increase our debt due to lusting for more material possessions, it may be sinful. Now don't beat yourself up if you have debt because of a desire to keep up with your neighbors. If that is a challenge for you, just take it to the Lord. He will help us when we seek His help.

Although I covered credit cards in my previous chapter, this is a good time to look at them again. We are under attack every day to acquire a new credit card. Institutions and outlets hit us with promotions in the mail and when we are making a purchase at a local retailer. It is so easy to put a purchase on a credit card. It seems like we do not even need money at the time of purchase.

Now here comes the worst part of having debt on a credit card: Remember if we decide to make the minimum payment amount each month, it could take more than twenty-five years to pay our balance off. That is why I recommend not to use credit cards if we are not able to pay off the entire amount we charge each month. Credit card use requires a disciplined life.

There may come a time when our debt is far beyond our ability to even make our minimum payment amounts. What options do we have? If we stop making any payments at all, we will be harassed by our creditors. In addition to that, we could get a court-ordered garnishment of our wages each month. This will harm our credit score.

May I suggest you do something that may seem a little ridiculous? I have seen it to be successful with some of those who I have helped get out of debt. Call your creditors and tell them about the financial trials you are going through. Let them know you are not able to make the payments on your debt. Ask them if they will reduce your debt or even forgive it.

Now before you think I must be crazy; I want to tell you about a person who did what I just suggested. This person had several large credit card balances and five or six personal loans. After he called all of his creditors and requested what I suggested he was shocked at the results. Nearly 1/3 of his debt was canceled. The interest rates on the remaining debts were all reduced. With all of these changes he was able to start paying off his remaining debt.

This reminds me of a few very important words I have read in the Bible that apply to this situation. You have not because you ask not.

This is a true story and we give all the credit (pun intended) to the Lord for what happened. There is no guarantee this will happen to you but it might be worth trying.

We all know about companies that offer credit counseling and debt-reduction plans. My suggestion is to investigate these companies prior to using them. Some are good but others may increase your debt problems.

As a banker I had customers who could not pay their financial obligations for various reasons. There were those who had no other option but to file bankruptcy. The "B" word always brings forth a plethora of concerns. Those concerns are valid and require legal assistance. Do not consider bankruptcy unless you seek qualified legal counsel.

As a Christian there are some issues that need to be addressed when we are considering filing bankruptcy. First, we must understand bankruptcy may not be a sin it is a legal option our country has provided for those who need help. It should never be used as a tool to hide illegal actions or to take advantage of our legal system. I am not recommending bankruptcy, yet in some cases it may be a proper action to take in order to reorganize our debts.

In order to help those who desire to live debt-free we can look at a few debt reduction ideas. They may not be new to you.

1. For the next twenty-four hours, look at your spending choices. Will you stop at a convenience store to buy something you don't really need? Will you go out to eat or eat at home? Are you thinking of going shopping to buy something you need or just want?

2. Decide if you are committed to be debt-free.

3. Keep in touch with your creditors. Let them know if you are in trouble with your finances. Talk to them and keep them up to date. As a banker for fourteen years, I could always be of greater help to someone the sooner I was made aware of a problem.

4. Contact a credit counseling service (check out their references). Many times they are able to get interest rates reduced or waived.

5. Start a plan to pay off your loans or credit cards beginning with the smallest balance first.

Following is an illustration of this type of debt reduction:

LOAN BALANCE PAYMENTS

Loan #1: $340.00   Monthly Minimum: $20.00
Pay off Loan #1 as fast as you are able.

Loan #2: $510.00   Minimum Payment: $ 25.00
When Loan #1 is paid off, pay $45 a month on Loan #2

Loan #3: $795.00   Minimum Payment: $30.00
When Loan #2 is paid off, pay $75 a month on Loan #3.

Loan #4: $2,300.00   Minimum Payment: $80.00
When Loan #3 is paid off, pay $155 a month on Loan #4.

Loan #5: $7,400.00   Minimum Payment: $260.00
When Loan #4 is paid off, pay $415 a month on Loan #5.

Loan #6 - Mortgage: $120,000.00 – Minimum Payment: $1,000.00

When Loan #5 is paid off, pay $1415 a month on Loan #6.
At this point, I would refinance the first mortgage with a ten

or fifteen year, no-fee loan. This depends on the current interest rates.

6. Call your credit card lenders and ask them to reduce your interest rate. Your chances are better than fifty percent they will.

7. Transfer credit card balances to special credit card rate offerings that never increase your loan balance.

8. Stop use of credit cards if you can't pay off the balanced owed each month.

9. Determine what you spend every month. Don't forget the non-monthly expenses, for example, car repairs, car insurance, car license plates, emergency contingencies and Christmas gifts. Without doing this, you will never begin to control expenses. We can't become debt-free or start saving until we accomplish this step.

10. Take a step every month toward debt-free living. It will not happen overnight, but overnight you can decide to make it happen.

11. Stop impulse purchases—the items we buy without prior planning.

12. Look at your current debt and payments and determine how long it will take to get out of debt. Try to make more than the minimum payment.

13. Accept the fact that discipline in our spending habits may be the only thing we need to become debt-free. Chapter Sixteen covers the topic of discipline.

Before you continue to the next chapter repeat this prayer: "Lord, I can see myself being debt-free. With your help, Lord, I call forth those things that are not as though they are. I will use the suggestions in this chapter to help me experience the joy of debt-free living. In Jesus' name I pray."

NOTES:
Start your debt reducing plan below.

_____

_____

_____

_____

_____

_____

_____

_____

_____

_____

_____

_____

_____

_____

_____

_____

_____

_____

_____

_____

Enjoy the goodness of God and be
thankful for all His blessings.

*Because the Lord disciplines the one he loves,
and he chastens everyone he accepts as his son.*
~ Hebrews 12:6 (NIV)

This could be the most important chapter in the book.

My experience has shown me that financial success depends on these four conditions:

1. Trust God with your finances.

2. Establish your tithe and give offerings to the work of the Lord.

3. Control spending habits.

4. Colossians. 3:23 (NKJV) reads: *Whatever you do, do it heartily.*

CHAPTER 8

Control Spending

MOST PEOPLE TELL me they run out of money before the end of each month. Some say they make enough money but they do not know where it all goes. For anyone who may feel this way, allow me to tell you a story about my own children.

When our kids were very young, say five or six years old, my wife and I tried to teach them a concept we hoped would stick with them for life:

Enjoy the goodness of God and be thankful for all His blessings.

When one of our children would ask for money to buy something, I would ask them how much they needed and what they wanted to buy. After they gave me a good reason I usually gave them the money they needed. It was usually a couple of dollars for something they saw on television or in a store. Those of you who raised or have small children understand this type of request.

A few days after I gave our children the money I would ask them if they were still enjoying the thing they bought with the money I had given them.

Most of the time they had forgotten what they bought and would ask me if they could have more money to buy something else. That is when I would attempt to explain the importance of being thankful for what they had received and not to take for granted the blessings of the Lord.

Now, some may think I was a little naïve in trying to teach our children this lesson at such an early age. I disagree with that type of thinking.

The word of God directs us to train our children in the way they should think and act. As parents we are being naïve if we don't believe that our children are aware of when they must be thankful and when they are being greedy.

By the way, I don't believe in the tradition of giving an allowance to children without them being responsible for performing certain work assignments around the house. I believe in faithfulness, and we should bless or reward our children for their faithfulness to their assigned responsibilities.

Too many times an allowance is something we give regardless of our children's faithfulness. Think about it. Our kids feel the allowance is something we owe them. They may feel they do not have to earn it. Some of you may not agree with me on this. However, America's children are being taught that their parents owe them whether they perform their daily responsibilities or not.

Children must be taught at an early age that they must earn the money they get. In addition to that they need to evaluate how and what they purchase with their money. Teaching our children good spending habits will bless them throughout their life.

Let's take a closer look at our spending habits. Following is a list of the most common things to consider when faced with making good spending decisions:

1. Look at your list of monthly expenses. Determine what are needs, wants or desires. A complete list includes non-monthly expenses, car repairs, and gifts (see Chapter Five).

2. Speak to your spouse, a good friend, or a family member about your spending decisions. Get their advice.

3. Record how you spend money, for example, when and how much. You don't have to record every dime, but record thirty days of spending.

4. Understand the value of Hebrews 12:6 and 11(NKJV): *For whom the Lord loves, He chastens and scourges every son whom He receives.* Verse 11: *Now no chastening seems to be joyful for the present, but painful; nevertheless, afterward it yields the peaceful fruit of righteousness to those who have been trained by it.*

As a pastor I would tell my congregation, I love it when the

EXPERIENCE THE JOY OF DEBT-FREE LIVING - David C. Friend

Lord disciplines me. First, because it proves to me He loves me. Second, because it yields righteousness and I will profit from His correction.

My suggestions about making spending decisions are basically asking you to live within your means. What does it mean to live within your means? Simply put, it means to spend only what you make.

The American way is to live above our means. Far too many want to have it now, to let others think they have more than they actually possess. Living above their means aka income, is typical. I call it false or fake prosperity. It's a lack of being content. I believe that over 50% of those I have counseled in the area of money, live above their income. This means they spend more than they make. It is as simple as that.

In my counseling sessions I discovered overspending was $300 to $1,000 a month. That spending was being covered with use of new loans or credit cards.

However, from my years of banking experience, it was interesting that wealthy customers spent less than they earn. This means they live below their means. Some would say they live within their means because they have more income to spend. I call it below their means because they choose to spend below what they could spend. In addition to that they save or invest their excess income.

A friend of mine sells luxury cars. He told me more than eighty percent of the people buying these cars cannot afford them. But, they are willing to go deep into debt and lose thousands of dollars on their purchase so they could appear wealthy. He said only one out of seven cars he sells with a sales price more than $50,000 is purchased by people who can afford them.

The following page is what I refer to as: Stair Steps to Financial Failure or Steps to Debt-Free Living. As you read the graph on the next page, try to imagine which step you are on, and in which direction your finances are going.

How We Step into Financial Failure

I want it now. I need to
treat myself, so why
wait to pay cash.

Blame my circumstances.
The boss doesn't like me.
I never get a break.

I Impulse buy.
Let others
control my spending.

Buying to feel good.
After all, I work
and I deserve this.

Thinking budgeting
is for losers.

Stair Steps to Debt-free Living
Read from bottom to top. It is like digging out of a hole.

Live debt-free.

See yourself being debt-free.

Reduce spending.

Determine how much you spend.

"Accept discipline."
~ Hebrews 12:6

Decide to Change – Your Plan Has Not Worked

It is never too late to control spending. Several years ago, a man nearing retirement made an appointment to see me about setting up a budget and expense plan. As we discussed his concerns, he told me although he had made more than $100,000 a year for a couple of decades, he did not have a savings account. His mortgage was approximately the appraised value of his home, therefore he did not have any equity. Because of this he did not know how he could ever expect to retire.

We set out on a plan to determine how much he spent every month, including the non-monthly items. We discovered he was spending about $3,000 a month in miscellaneous expenses. He had a couple of large loan payments but overall, if he would change and change quickly, there was still time to recover.

In only a couple of months, this gentleman made many corrections to his spending. He sold an expensive car and reduced his overall payments. He gained control of his spending habits by setting up a budget. Then he made a decision to live within this budget. He soon became on his way to debt-free living.

You might say if you made more than $100,000 a year, it would be easy to do what this person did. That is easy to say but not always easy to do. It takes little effort to evaluate someone else but it may be extremely difficult to evaluate yourself.

I have discovered if we can't deal with our spending habits when we make little, it may be more difficult when we make more. In addition to that, it will only get harder the longer you wait and the older you get. I believe if we are unfaithful with little, we will be unfaithful with much.

As I close this chapter, think of how we can teach proper spending habits to our children. Maybe the way we teach them to conserve is a lesson for us. It's kind of funny how we look at our children at times. If we look close enough, we can see ourselves in them.

When our children want a toy, they try to justify the purchase. They say, "Mom, Dad, I've been good," or, "I'll be better." If you tell them you can't afford to buy the toy right now, their response might be, "You have money, just write a check." We laugh and say they don't understand that having checks or credit cards does not mean we can afford to buy something.

Let's look at ourselves when we want something. We know it is not in the budget, we know we should not buy it at this time, but we drag out the credit cards and say we can buy it now. After all, we have a credit card. We justify to ourselves what we laugh about in our children. The next time we tell our children "not now" or "not at this time" let's be sure we have learned something from the way we teach them.

As we continue to claim debt-free living, we will discover we may not need more income to become debt-free. Our spending habits can always improve. We can start today on making good spending decisions. Please don't wait. Just do it.

My prayer for you is: "Heavenly Father, we all need your

help in determining what we should spend the income in which we have been blessed. Help us to understand the differences between our needs, wants and desires.

"You promised in your word to provide for our needs. We thank you for that promise. Help us to avoid impulse purchases. These will always make a negative impact on our budget. Thank you for your instructions in Chapter 3 in the book of Proverbs on how we should handle our finances. We need your help to carry out your biblical plan for our finances.

"We surrender our thoughts to your instructions. May we experience the joy of debt-free living. Thank you for your instruction and guidance. Thank you for your Holy Spirit, who will help us in all of our financial decisions. In Jesus' name we pray. Amen."

NOTES:
List your plans to spend less.

If only I would budget or spend more time on controlling my spending, and less time thinking about making more money.

The fallacy is, it always takes two incomes to live today.

Decide not to live below God's standard of living for you.

CHAPTER 9

More Income:
Not necessarily the Answer

MAKING MORE MONEY might be like taking a painkiller for your body. It fixes the problem temporarily, but it does not tell you what caused the problem. For years I've heard the following statement: "If only I made more money." It's true that in some cases making more money may be necessary. However, the majority of times people should say: "If only I would budget or spend more time on controlling my spending and less time thinking about making more money."

An instant increase in income may not be a blessing or the answer to our financial need. We have all seen or read about those who became wealthy overnight and how their lives become a disaster. One of the reasons the prosperity message is so popular is because many believe it's a quick fix to their financial woes.

Before we decide more money is the answer, let's ask

ourselves a few questions:

1. Is there a shortage of money, or do we have a wrong attitude toward spending?

2. Do we desire more money to feed our relentless desire for material possessions?

3. Have we ever considered the question, "How much income is enough?"

These are not popular questions today. Another unpopular question is: do both the husband and wife work full-time outside the home to meet their needs or to get a bigger house, second car, better clothes, nicer furniture, or whatever they want?

There is a fallacy people are talking about today all over this wonderful country of ours. The fallacy is that it always takes two incomes to live today. Now stay with me. I realize there are circumstances where two incomes are necessary for a specific period of time. Illness or economic conditions may require a need for two incomes. However, sometimes the need for two incomes is only a desire to increase a standard of living.

Every week I meet couples who are living on one income.

Granted, some do not always have the money to get the little extras. If we believe the fallacy that it's impossible for a family to live on one income, we are saying our God is not able to help us. Yet, the book of Ephesians 3:20 (NKJV) tells us: *God is able to do exceedingly abundantly above anything we can imagine or even think.*

If we examine our spending attitudes and look closely at the actual cost of a second car, nursery costs for our children, or costs for extra clothes, we will quickly discover it may not be a shortage of money as much as it is a decision of priorities in our families today. Before you get mad at me or throw this book in the trash, maybe, just maybe, our God is able to do something we cannot imagine or even think.

I suggest that married couples with children live within the income of the person who desires to work outside the home. Our children often face greater challenges today than we did growing up. Because of that, if at all possible, one of the parents should try to stay home with them. I realize in today's society, the primary income might be that of the man or the woman. It is up to the parents to decide who brings home the income.

I understand many will need help to figure out a way to make this happen. It may take a year or two to accomplish it but, at least you could try, if it is what you want for your family. The ideas in this book will help if you give them a chance.

In this chapter, I want to focus on the question: "Is more income the answer to live debt-free?" As I have previously said, "More money will not always be the answer."

When we make $50,000 a year, let's live within that amount. As the Lord blesses, and our income increases to $60,000 a year, why must we continue to increase spending? I suggest we increase spending by only 10% of our increase in income. Example: If your current income goes up 10%, increase your standard of living by 1 percent. Use the other 9% to save and pay off debt.

It is not a coincidence that most of the millionaires in our country today live a life-style below their income. Years ago, I met a successful businessman who decided to set his standard of living at $100,000 a year. His income increased to $200,000, yet he left his standard of living at $100,000. He continued this plan until he was making over a million dollars annually. At this point, he felt it was time to increase his spending to $200,000 a year.

I can hear your comments now. You are saying, "If I had $100,000 a year, I would be happy to set my standard of living at that amount and leave it there." My question for you is: "What would you do when your income increases?"

My experience tells me if we won't control spending with a $50,000 income, we probably won't control it at $100,000.

It may seem a little strange to think that more money might not be the answer. It may also seem strange to not automatically spend more when we make more. What I want you to understand is we must think differently than we have in the past in order to live debt-free. We must develop an attitude of discipline. The result of this type of discipline will lead to living a debt-free life.

It is important to understand that the Lord wants us to prosper. I believe He wants us to live debt-free. In addition to that, He wants us to live according to His standard of living. The Word of God even tells us to prosper. The 3 John 2 (NKJV) scripture reads: *Beloved, I pray that you may prosper in all things and be in health, just as your soul prospers.*

Stay with me on this. If you want to live debt-free and have freedom from always needing more income, then go back and examine the three points mentioned previously at the beginning of this chapter. I realize today more income may be needed to meet your needs. However, when our spending is under control, and we know how much it takes to live each month based on the entire year's expenses, then, and only then, will we be on the road to debt-free living.

Please accept this prayer: "Father may the reader of this chapter understand the principle that more income is not always the answer. Without controlling our spending habits we will never be set free from the bondage of debt. Your word Lord tells us to be sensitive in how we spend our money. May we seek your direction in our financial decisions.

"Continually increasing our spending will never bring forth our desire to be debt-free. Heavenly Father, help us to establish a budget and live within that budget. May the Holy Spirit help us to evaluate the importance of every expenditure.

"Lord, we desire to improve our process of determining every spending decision. With your help we will be successful and experience a debt-free life. As we read Proverbs Chapter 3 reveal to us how it applies to our daily experiences with money. Thank you for the help you have provided through you word. May our finances be a blessing to us and to others. In Jesus' name we pray. Amen."

NOTES:
List what you might cut in your spending.

_____

_____

_____

_____

_____

_____

_____

_____

_____

_____

_____

_____

_____

_____

_____

_____

_____

_____

_____

Read God's Word. Now do His word.

Where we are financially is the sum total of all the financial decisions we have made to date.

It is poor judgment to countersign another's note, to become responsible for his debts.
~ Proverbs 17:18 (NKJV)

CHAPTER 10

Freedom in Decisions

ONE DAY I stopped by a convenience store to get a quick cup of coffee. A young lady working behind the counter was complaining about her job. She said to a co-worker, "They only pay me $10.00 an hour." You could see her frustration and anger. A young man walked up behind me and said to her, "Did you get your new shoes?" The young lady smiled and put her foot up on the counter and said, "Yes, do you like them?" Then she made a powerful statement revealing her attitude about money and spending: "Not bad for only $128.00." All of a sudden I had this hollow feeling in my stomach. One moment she was complaining about earning only $10.00 an hour, the next moment she was showing excitement about a purchase she would have to work almost two days to acquire.

Talk about needing a financial makeover on financial

decisions. As I walked out of the store, all I could think about was what had brought this young woman to this decision? What was her thought process? What caused her to feel a need to make that purchase?

When we are facing a financial decision, we need to stop and think about how this may affect our finances. You might want to think about how long you will have to work to pay for what you are about to purchase. As a person who believes in prayer, I like to pray before I venture out to buy something. Then I like to listen for direction from the Holy Spirit. By that I mean I want to think about how I feel about my purchasing plans. Wait until I receive peace. If I do not have peace, I will not buy anything.

That goes along with the idea of; when in doubt don't. The Apostle Paul gave us instructions for making decisions in Philippians 4:6 – 7 (NKJV): *Be anxious for nothing, but in everything by prayer and supplication, with thanksgiving, let your requests be made known to God; and the peace of God, which surpasses all understanding, will guard your hearts and minds through Christ Jesus.*

Peace means we are trusting the Lord for the decision. Peace is not what you get when you try to manipulate your circumstances to get what you want. Peace is something we must have whether we get the answer we want or not. Anytime we are thinking about spending the money we have worked hard to obtain, we need to ask the Holy Spirit to help us with our decision.

Look into the scriptures to find help from the Lord. As I

have mentioned previously, my suggestion is, to read Chapter 3 of the book of Proverbs. Then look up every reference to making decisions in the entire book of Proverbs. Underline them in your Bible. After we pray and have read God's directions on making good decisions, we will be prepared to make the proper decision. When we have peace, then we can take action and make that financial decision.

Following is a list of steps I believe will help us make Spirit-led financial decisions:

1. Don't allow others to make decisions for you. Seek God and godly counsel. However, you must make the final decision.

2. Avoid speculation. Do not decide to spend money or borrow money today that will require hoped-for income in the future. Proverbs 27:12 (NKJV): *A prudent man foresees evil and hides (protects) himself; the simple pass on and are punished.*

3. Only lend money to people if you can afford to lose it. A loan to another person is an extremely risky decision. This applies to Christians, family, and non-believers. I realize we must help our family and friends, but adding a loan to your relationship could be a time bomb.

4. Only invest money if it represents excess funds above your budget needs. Buying speculative investments with your daily budget money almost assures financial disaster.

5. Don't put our budget into financial bondage and expect

the Lord to bail us out. Buying a new car with a payment larger than we can afford today, based on a potential pay raise, is like gambling in Las Vegas. Sooner or later, we will lose.

6. When buying a car consider the impact the decision will have on our spouse, children, church, tithing, and offerings. Buying a luxury car that would keep our child from going to a Christian school or cause us to stop tithing is a poor decision.

7. Never guarantee another person's loan. Proverbs 17:18 (TLB): *It is poor judgment to countersign another's note, to become responsible for his debts.*

I've often said I would not co-sign for my own mother. Read on! Think of this: What if I cosign for Mom and she forgets to make the payment or the check gets lost in the mail? Either way, she meant well, but now the loan becomes past due and my credit is affected. We have placed pressure on our relationship and it was my fault for not listening to the word of God. I suggest we follow the Word of God and not co-Sign. This does not mean that I would not help my mother. I would not let my mother go in need.

Therefore, if a family member or a friend has a need and you have prayed for direction and believe you must help them, then my suggestion is to give them the money. If you don't have it, borrow the money yourself and make the payments. They can pay you back later if they are able.

8. Never make an impulse purchase that costs more than $20 without thinking and praying. If it was a planned purchase, and it's more than $20, then go ahead, as long as you are at peace about the purchase. If in doubt, don't buy. God is not a God of doubt or a God of impulse. Impulse buying shows a lack of discipline. Retailers line the check-out counters with impulse items in order to entice us to buy more and pray less.

9. Prepare for an emergency. That is why we are supposed to have savings accounts. Too many prepare for an emergency with a credit card and not with a savings plan.

Often someone will ask me about a decision they need to make concerning their finances. My first question to them is, "What does the Word of God say you should do?" As Christians we must always consult God's Word before making financial decisions. I guarantee you the word of God addresses every decision we need to make.

Where we are financially today is the sum total of all the financial decisions we have made to date. Just think of that statement. Every time we buy something, it affects something else in our budget. Always understand when we spend a dollar, it is gone and cannot be used to save, pay off debt, or give help to others.

To have freedom in our financial decisions and to become debt-free is not a quick fix. We can't put it in the microwave or take a pill. Freedom from debt is a life-style decision. We must take personal responsibility for our past financial decisions and decide to make good ones in the future.

At the end of this chapter I have a page where you can list the financial decisions you need to make. Before you make that list take a moment and pray. Ask the Holy Spirit to help you make a complete list. After you make your list make a comment in the margin as to whether it is a need, want or desire.

This list will be a major step in moving toward your goal of debt-free living.

My prayer for you is: "Lord, we need your help in making decisions. May we be sensitive to the still quiet voice of the Holy Spirit to help us in every area of our finances. Thank you for caring about the decisions we need to make. May our decisions help us to become debt-free. In Jesus' name we pray. Amen."

NOTES:
List Financial decisions you are facing.

_____

_____

_____

_____

_____

_____

_____

_____

_____

_____

_____

_____

_____

_____

_____

_____

_____

_____

_____

_____

_____

If you really want to tithe you can.
The word of God tells us to test God in
our giving and see if He won't bless us
in return.

Give and it will be given unto you…
~ Luke 6:38 (NKJV)

*For My thoughts are not your thoughts, nor
are your ways my ways says the Lord.*
~ Isaiah 55:8 (NKJV)

CHAPTER 11

Give To Be Debt-Free

THIS WILL BE my favorite chapter.

Every time I get the opportunity to speak on giving something wonderful happens inside of me. It is difficult to explain but I get a feeling something miraculous is about to happen. Someone will be set free from the fear of giving. Someone will see how giving is the action they need to take in order to receive a blessing from the windows of heaven.

However, I understand this chapter may not be very popular to everyone. At first, I was not sure I should even write it so, here it goes. I promise to tell the truth, the whole truth, and nothing but the truth, so help me Lord.

First of all, giving or tithing does not make sense to the non-believer. To those who have not made Jesus Christ lord of their life, the thought of giving 10% of their income to their church seems a little ridiculous.

The world's concept of money is to work in order to build your wealth and to keep it all to yourself. Years ago I received a letter from a stockbroker. He said, "As we all know, it's not how much we make it is how much we keep." That statement has some merit however, keeping all we make is a grave mistake.

The Biblical concept of giving is to make money so we will have prosperity and abundance with the ability to provide for our needs and have enough to help others. As Christians, we know whatever we have, we must give it away and it will come back to us. Luke 6:38 (NKJV) reads: *Give and it will be given unto you; good measure, pressed down, shaken together, and running over will be put into your bosom. For with the same measure that you use, it will be measured back to you.*

If you have a problem with this concept of giving first in order to receive, you must read Malachi 3:6 – 10 (NKJV). This is where the Word of God tells us to test God and see if He won't bless us in return. I challenge you to do just that. Decide in your heart to trust the Lord and take the step of faith and decide to become a generous giver and tither.

Regardless of how much we give we can never out give God. It's sad to say this but most Christians do not trust God with their money. From my experience as a banker for fourteen years in lending to churches and helping churches obtain financing, I have consistently discovered usually less than 10% of God's people are tithers. Yet, 100% of God's people want the blessing of God in their finances.

To those who tithe 10% of their income to their church, the next paragraph is common knowledge to you. But to those of you who have decided to just now become a tither we need to explain how you will get there?

It's wonderful when the Holy Spirit speaks to us to give. Most Christians want to give, but they don't know how to start. Where do they find the money? Some tell us to just start tithing. Write the check today.

What they are saying is to ignore your current obligations, your written promise to pay. I totally disagree with the suggestion. As Christians, the world looks at our character very closely. Deciding to give your money to the church instead of paying our debt is a poor witness. God will help us to do better than that. Let me suggest we cannot only become a tither, but we can also pay our bills and honor our word to those we owe money.

Let me give you some things we must do when the Holy Spirit touches our heart and convicts us to start giving tithes and offerings. If we really want to tithe, we can. Most people are able to become tithers within a few weeks. It will open up a lifetime of financial freedom and debt-free living. Here are a couple of suggestions on how to become a tither:

1. Set up an expense plan, review (Chapter Five). This plan will show you where your money is going.

2. Review your list of expenses and determine if you are

spending your income the best way possible.

Let me give you an example involving a young couple who came in to see me many years ago about how to become tithers. They really wanted to tithe, but they believed it would be next to impossible.

The couple earned $3,000.00 a month and thought the $300.00 to tithe was nowhere to be found. Does this sound familiar to you? Let me remind you they said their number one desire was to become tithers. As they sat down to talk with me, I noticed the two coffee lattes in their hands.

Their children were eating candy bars and they had a several bags of chips that were about empty. I asked them the following question, "How often do you get those snacks?" The husband said, "Well everyday." Then he went on to say, "You see pastor, we work hard and we need to treat ourselves to something, so every day we go down to the coffee shop and buy these treats." He wanted to change the subject so he said, "Let's get down to business." So I did.

I totaled up the costs of their "treats." It was costing them more than $10.00 a day. It's interesting that 30 days times $10.00 equaled the amount they needed to become tithers. The "treats" they were buying were robbing them of becoming tithers. They already had what they needed to become tithers. Today many couples spend money at yogurt or coffee shops that could be a source of funds that could be used to start tithing.

I realize my example of $3,000 a month may seem small today. However, whether we make $3,000 a month or $10,000 every month, this example holds true.

Now I believe it is okay to treat our family to something every once in a while. However, there are more reasonable ways to do that than go to a local specialty snack shop. A better treat would be to go to a park or walking trail and take something less expensive with you. Besides after you start to tithe to your church, I believe your finances will be blessed and you will be able to enjoy a treat. That treat will come from the Lord, because He will bless you when you put Him first in your finances.

I have seen financial blessings occur in my own life and in the lives of so many others when they gave of their finances to the work of the Lord.

According to Malachi 3:6–10 (NKJV) by starting to tithe, any couple or individual could pour the foundation of a sound financial plan based on God's Word.

Let's get back to the couple in my office. As soon as I pointed out their miracle breakthrough to tithing was being spent daily at the snack store, this couple became very silent. We prayed together and they thanked me for the time we had spent together. They knew what had to be done. If they really, truly, honestly wanted to tithe, they could. I'll never know if they became tithers. However, many others have become tithers because they could relate to this story.

Let me ask you to think about this: Is your tithe in your

treats, snacks, or lunch money? Is your tithe in the car payment you make each month? Are you robbing God because of the size of your monthly house payment or the maintenance or utilities on your home?

Without a doubt, I believe the Lord wants us to tithe. I also believe He is not against us having a nice car, a beautiful home, vacations, and an abundant amount of money from which we can enjoy our life and yet still be able to give. If we really want to tithe, we can. We can tithe and still have nice things. We can have both of these in our life. We do not have to choose between tithing or enjoying life.

We put limits on the Lord when we believe if we tithe we will not be able to buy anything. We serve a God without limits. Isaiah 55:8–9 (NKJV) reads: *For My thoughts are not your thoughts, nor are your ways my ways, says the Lord. For as the heavens are higher than the earth, so are my ways higher than your ways, and my thoughts than your thoughts.*

From this scripture, we can see the Lord has thoughts and ways for us to prosper financially. So, let's yield to His ways. Let's establish the tithe and test the Lord to see how His ways, will pour out a blessing we cannot even contain.

We must decide to become a giver to the work of the Lord. In our church services we must believe giving is one of the highlights every week. We can't all sing or preach or go overseas to start a mission but we can all decide to give. Look forward to opportunities to give. We should approach giving with an understanding that God's thoughts should be our thoughts and His ways should be our ways.

In our church, when I said it's time we receive the tithes and offerings, the congregation would applaud and rejoice in being able to give and help the work of the Lord. That always reminded me of 2 Corinthians 9:7 (NKJV): *So let each one give as he purposes in his heart, not grudgingly or of necessity; for God loves a cheerful giver.*

Never forget, we can't out give the Lord. He has given us eternal life through the gift of His son Jesus Christ when He was crucified on the cross. When we have freedom to give, we are free financially. Being financially free will bring forth freedom from debt. If you are not tithing to your church, start today to develop a plan to tithe. You can and you will be blessed, and you will be free through your trust in God. The Bible tells us those the Lord sets free are free indeed.

My prayer for you is: "Lord, may we step out in faith to give of our finances to your church. This will provide for the needs of others in our community. In turn you have promised to bless us when we bless others. Thank you for the opportunity help those in need through the ministries of the local church. In Jesus' name we pray. Amen."

NOTES:
List where your tithing may be hidden.

_____

_____

_____

_____

_____

_____

_____

_____

_____

_____

_____

_____

_____

_____

_____

_____

_____

_____

_____

_____

_____

_____

_____

_____

He who trusts the Lord will prosper.
~ Proverbs 28:25 (NKJV)

A faithful man will abound with blessings,
but he who hastens to be rich will
not go unpunished.
~ Proverbs 28:20 (NKJV)

Trust in the Lord with all your heart and lean
not on your own understanding.
~ Proverbs 3:4 (NKJV)

CHAPTER 12

Financial Success

MOST PEOPLE WANT financial success in their life. We hear the phrase Financial Independence over and over again from investment counselors, brokerage firms radio and television ads. As Christians, we know our God desires to bless us, but we must never desire independence from His plan and still expect His blessing. God is our source of prosperity.

If we believe God is our source then we must be dependent on His word for our financial success. We could study dozens of ways to obtain financial success and become financially independent. However, unless we use the principles for good decision making found in God's word we will never experience dependence on God. I have prepared these six keys to help you open the door to your financial success:

1. Avoid quick decisions. Proverbs 28:20 (NKJV) reads: *A*

faithful man will abound with blessings, but he who hastens to be rich will not go unpunished. We must always take time to decide. Don't be pushed by others to make a hasty decision.

2. Deal with integrity in all money matters. We have all heard the statement, "It's the principle, not the money," when there is a dispute in a financial issue. However, when we hear this it is usually the money. During the years I spent in real estate development, I experienced that comment on many occasions. Sometimes I would ask the question, "How much is the principle going to cost?" In every situation we had to come to a financial settlement.

Money is one of man's most personal possessions. Proverbs 28:6 (NKJV) reads: *Better is the poor who walks in his integrity than one perverse in his ways, though he be rich.* Integrity is always best. Integrity in our finances is not pretending or playing a game. Anytime we pretend to be someone we are not, we lack integrity.

3. Avoid conflict in settling money disputes if at all possible. A few times in my real estate development business I experienced conflict with how a transaction should be paid or how to settle financial disputes. One rule we operated by was to avoid legal action and settle the dispute even if it caused a financial loss.

Here are a couple of statements I learned years ago as a banker: "Your first loss is your best loss" and "Never put in good money after bad money." [authors unknown].

These statements tell us to settle a dispute as fast as we can and avoid adding to our potential loss.

One such potential conflict occurred with a Christian friend of mine. We went into a partnership and as business progressed, I was promised a large fee for overseeing a certain transaction. When the transaction was complete, my partner refused to pay my fee. He admitted he owed me the money but said he needed it more than I did. In addition, he was in serious need of money and wanted to break up our partnership. He asked me to pay back his $50,000 investment in our partnership, prior to its due date. Then he said if I did not do what he requested he would file a lawsuit against my company.

At first I was irritated, upset and a little disappointed. Because of the agreement, I could have delayed or even sued for my rights. However, I thought of the statement, "Your first loss is your best loss." My wife and I prayed and wanted to know what the word of God would tell us to do. We decided to do what we read in the Bible regardless of how it sounded to us.

We read 2 Timothy 2:23 (NKJV): *But avoid foolish and ignorant disputes, knowing that they generate strife.*

My wife and I decided to settle the dispute with our Christian friend. We had to borrow money to pay the $50,000, and we split up the partnership. I forgave the dispute over the fee owed to me, and my friend and I went our separate ways. We did not split with anger, hate, or disagreement.

Some of you may be wondering how all of that turned out. As Paul Harvey would have said, "Here is the rest of the story."

Within thirty days, the property I bought from the partnership sold. Previously that property had not received any calls or interest from anyone for several months. The real estate market was slow and in decline. Not only did I get back the $50,000 I gave my previous partner, but I made enough profit to cover the lost fee and receive a $100,000 profit.

The word of God told us to settle disputes quickly and we did. God was faithful to our decision to trust in His word.

Now I realize there are times when you might face a dispute that will require legal help. But even in that situation, try to settle a dispute quickly. Before taking legal action, seek God's word. Before meeting with someone who is in dispute with you pray for favor from the Lord. I have done that and have been blessed.

Because of looking to God's Word for our direction and having faith in His ways, I was never sued or had to file a lawsuit against anyone to settle a transaction. That covered over thirty years of doing business in real estate. We give all the credit to our God and His advice in His word.

4. Always be honest and upfront with people. In any transaction, both sides should profit. It is always right to do what is right. Proverbs 28:13 (NKJV) reads: *He who covers his transgression will not prosper.*

5. Place our trust in God. The Bible tells us in Proverbs 28:25 (NKLV): *He who trusts the Lord will prosper.* His Word also tells us in Proverbs 3:5 (NKJV): *Trust in the Lord with all your heart and lean*

not on your own understanding. God does not earn our trust, we must earn His. The battle most Christians have with this scripture is, *"Lean not on your own understanding."* Operating with only our understanding has limits. We all know God's understanding is without limits.

6. Avoid every form of greed. Watch our motives in buying anything.

Ask yourself if the financial decision you are considering is based on need or greed. Only you are able to answer the question. A short time ago, I took my wife to a Broadway play presented here in Phoenix. It was a last-minute decision to buy the tickets, so the seat selections were not very good. The decision I had to make was to pay $60 for a seat three or four seats in from the outside edge of the row, or to pay $15 for seats on the outside edge of the row. The ticket salesperson told me the view would be somewhat obstructed in the far, deep-right corner of the stage. We had seen the play before, so I did not feel we would miss much. As it turned out, we didn't miss anything. We did not have any view restrictions.

You may wonder why I'm telling you this story and what does it have to do with financial success and becoming debt-free. Let me just point out every time we decide to spend money it will make an impact on our finances. Once we spend our hard-earned money we can never get it back. Be sure what we purchase is made with the proper motives. We must decide to never buy something in an effort to impress others.

Now back to my story about our trip to see a play. Well, I will admit at first I felt a little bit like a cheapskate. But that is not the point I want to focus on. As we sat on the end of the row, people would stop, look around, and make comments about their better seats and they had paid for good seats toward the center. We found it funny that those who had paid significantly more than we did were sitting very close to us. As a matter of fact, most of them were only a few seats away.

Let me ask you this:

Do we spend money to appear to be something we are not? Do we have to drive a car with a luxury hood ornament in order to feel successful? Are the financial decisions we make affected by our need to look affluent?

In summarizing this chapter: What is success? Is it having more possessions than others? The answers to those questions are based on the actions we take to be successful. Do we avoid quick financial decisions? Do we always put integrity first? Are we honest and avoid conflict? Is our trust in God and do we keep greed from motivating our decisions?

We must never forget that real success is how we live in our walk with our Lord. The result of serving the Lord in His plan for our finances will be a life with financial freedom. Freedom to live debt-free.

My prayer for you is: "Heavenly Father, I believe you desire to see your followers experience success. The greatest success we will ever attain is to accept you as our Lord and Savior. From that point on, we become your heirs, enabling us to receive blessings in every area of our life. Help us to always pursue your plans for financial success. Thank you in advance for future success in our finances. May that success provide for a life of debt-free living. In Jesus' name I pray. Amen."

NOTES:
What does being successful mean to you?

_____

_____

_____

_____

_____

_____

_____

_____

_____

_____

_____

_____

_____

_____

_____

_____

_____

_____

We do not have to choose between
spiritual prosperity and financial prosperity.
We can have both.

*But seek first the kingdom of God and His
righteousness, and all these things
shall be added to you.*
~ Matthew 6:33 (NKJV)

*And you shall remember the Lord your God,
for it is He who gives you power to get wealth.*
~ Deuteronomy 8:18 (NKJV)

CHAPTER 13

Spiritual or Financial Prosperity

TODAY THE MESSAGE of financial prosperity is a hot topic. Whenever I prepare a message about financial prosperity, the interest is well-received. When I would announce I will be speaking about financial prosperity, the attendance of the service would increases significantly. We know the financial prosperity message has merit. If a financial prosperity teaching is based on the Word of God, it is life changing. However, every financial message must start with a focus on spiritual prosperity.

Jesus said in Matthew 6:33 (NKJV): *But seek first the kingdom of God and His righteousness, and all these things shall be added to you.*

If we are not careful, a message of financial prosperity will focus our attention on the gift of finances rather than the giver of every good and perfect gift. Look up James 1:17 (NKJV).

When we think about prosperity we must follow the following guidelines. Spiritual prosperity must always precede financial prosperity.

1. God is our source. Deuteronomy 8:18 (NKJV): *And you shall remember the Lord your God for it is He who gives you power to get wealth.* Never forget God is our source of financial gain. Everyone must place their trust in God and not in their financial plan. Spiritual growth will draw us closer to the Lord. The closer we get to God, the more we realize He is our source for financial prosperity.

2. Have the right motives. James 4:3 (NAS): *You ask and do not receive because you ask with wrong motives, so that you may spend it on your pleasure.* The Lord is concerned about our motives. Spiritual growth will establish the right motives in our finances. The Lord cannot trust us with financial gain if our motives are improper. Sometimes we have a difficult time trusting in God to bless us financially. I believe a bigger question is, "Can God trust us?" Can He trust us to do the right thing with a financial blessing? If we have experienced spiritual prosperity we are better prepared to do His will with His blessing.

3. Delight yourself in God. Psalm 37:4 (NAS) reads: *Delight yourself in the Lord and He will give you the desires of your heart.* We all want to receive the desires of our heart. The scripture says delight yourself in the Lord. It does not say delight yourself in your desires. Financial freedom along with living debt-free will happen when we delight ourselves in God. When we do this, our desires will line up with God's financial plan for us. Far too many

people delight in material gain, new homes, cars, second homes, vacations, and keeping up with the neighbors. Again, we must remember Matthew 6:33 (NKJV): *But seek first His kingdom and His righteousness and all these things shall be added to you.*

4. Prosper in all things. We do not have to choose between spiritual prosperity and financial prosperity. We can have them both. We know that because of what is written in 3 John 2 (NAS): *Beloved I pray that in all respects you may prosper and be in good health, just as your soul prospers.* The Lord wants us to prosper in all things. That includes things spiritual, physical, and financial. Once we decide to pursue spiritual growth, we will receive prosperity in every area.

Let me say that again. We do not have to choose between spiritual prosperity and financial prosperity. We can have them both. The road to every type of prosperity must be paved with spiritual growth.

Christians must acknowledge God is our source. We need proper motives to delight ourselves in God. A life focused primarily on financial prosperity with no concern for spiritual prosperity is a life out of focus. It's a life without financial freedom and usually never becomes debt-free.

Most individuals with financial problems believe the answer is more money. This is usually not the solution. The solution is being faithful with what we have. Luke 16:10 (NKJV) reads: *If you are faithful in little, you will be faithful with much.*

After working with thousands of individuals I have discovered that those who are faithful with little will be faithful with much. Conversely, those who are not faithful with little will not be faithful with much.

We must spend time in prayer seeking the Lord's will in our finances. Every person needs a scripture-based financial plan. When we establish a desire for spiritual growth, financial prosperity will soon follow. That is when we will live debt-free.

My prayer for you is: "Lord, thank you for always being faithful to us. May we desire to be faithful to you. The desire to be faithful will come when we desire to prosper spiritually. Help us to always place spiritual prosperity above financial prosperity. As we prosper spiritually every segment of our life will prosper. In Jesus' name I pray. Amen."

NOTES:
List examples of spiritual prosperity.

_____

_____

_____

_____

_____

_____

_____

_____

_____

_____

_____

_____

_____

_____

_____

_____

_____

_____

_____

_____

_____

We all trust in the Lord, or at least we all say we trust Him.

Everyone knows a budget is critical in marriage yet few have one.

Discipline in a couple's finances is the basis for healthy finances.

CHAPTER 14

Money and Marriage

THE SUBJECT OF money and marriage deserves far more than a chapter, however I will try and highlight the areas of great importance, which will help lead your marriage to live debt-free.

Today, many tell us money is the number one problem causing divorce. We know the Bible speaks more about money, possessions, materialism and the proper use or improper use of money than almost any other subject.

A simple review of a Bible Concordance on these issues will prove my point: The average married couple in the year 2017 owed more than $15,000 in credit card debt. With the good economy that year, it is a contradiction to see bankruptcies were nearly 800,000. There were more than 1,000,000 bankruptcies granted in the year 2014.

We need to ask ourselves: What is the cause of all these financial problems? Why do couples struggle with finances? Why are our couples getting deeper in debt with no plan to change? Let's work on the problem of debt. Ironically, the solution is found in my acronym: D.E.B.T.

Discipline

Energy

Budget

Trust

DISCIPLINE in a couple's finances is the basis for healthy finances. That applies to anyone. Proverbs 12:1 (NIV) reads: *Whoever loves discipline loves knowledge, but he who hates correction is stupid.*

Some Bible translations are direct, and this is one of them. A marriage without financial discipline is a marriage facing possible severe difficulty. As this translation points out, it's stupid to avoid correction, instruction and discipline. Money in a marriage without discipline is a soon coming financial tsunami.

Sooner or later financial woes will flood into our marriage and when it does, the marriage may be destroyed. Our financial failure impacts our children, friends, and family. The word discipline is so important, I dedicated the last chapter in this book to the benefit of discipline. To become debt-free will require discipline.

ENERGY exists in all marriages. The problem is, the energy may be spent in the wrong direction. Couples have energy to work, to have fun, go on vacations, bear children, and enjoy the physical rewards of marriage. The energy we use to shop for things like work, cars, furniture, homes, clothes, and material possessions is usually our biggest use of energy.

If we could direct, guide, or monitor some of our energy toward making sound financial decisions, we would surely see greater financial success. As couples, we should place our energy in praying together about our spending, in reading the Word of God and in seeking His help in financial decisions.

The energy we have to make money comes from the Lord. Deuteronomy 8:18 (NIV) reads: *But remember the Lord your God for it is He who gives you the ability to produce wealth.*

Energy is wonderful, yet it needs to be directed and brought under control. Couples should ask the Lord to direct them and agree together to focus some of their energy to become debt-free.

BUDGET. Everyone knows a budget is critical in marriage. Proverbs 16–9 (NKJV) reads: *A man's heart plans his way. But the Lord directs his steps.*

This shows the importance of making the effort to plan our finances through the tool of a budget. The budget is the place where a husband and wife come together to plan how they will use the income God provides. Doing a budget may be the only time a couple will sit down and plan the use of money.

My experience shows only five percent of the couples I've interviewed have had such a meeting. A well planned budget requires input by both the husband and wife. Both must openly discuss their wants, needs, and desires. Both must listen and put the others needs above their own personal wants, needs, and desires.

When it comes to spending, wives are often confronted by their husband for buying lots of little things for the home or for the children and when these purchases are not planned, they put pressure on the budget. On the other hand, traditionally, men are usually the ones who make the big spending decisions. A husband may argue with his wife over the $20 and $30 purchases she makes on the family or the house. Yet, the same men go out and buy a $55,000 recreation vehicle and put a $700 car payment on a budget that is struggling. I am not making that up. Obviously it does not happen in all marriages.

In marriage we come together as one. We are to make decisions together, pray together, have fun together, laugh together, and cry together. Let's work toward preparing a budget and living within it. There is little hope for couples to live debt-free without a plan of monitored spending. AKA, a budget.

TRUST. My favorite scripture about trust is found in Proverbs 3:5 (NKJV) reads: *Trust in the Lord with all your heart and lean not on your own understanding.* I realize I quote this quite often. But it is a scripture that must be part of our daily life.

Once, I interviewed a couple who were planning to get married. They wanted to know how to set up their finances from being single to being married. The first thing I suggested was to set up a joint checking account. When the guy heard my advice, he said, "How do I know I can trust her?" He wanted to marry her and yet it scared him to death to put his paycheck in the same account where she could write checks. How do you think that made her feel? It's obvious they had never discussed this issue.

We all know trust is vital in a marriage, both husband and wife must earn each other's trust. By the way, that couple decided to delay their wedding until they could work out the problem. About six months later they were married in our church. I thank the Lord they settled this issue before the wedding.

A marriage without trust is a marriage headed for failure. I've said this before but it is worth saying over and over again. We all trust the Lord, or at least we all say we trust Him. The bigger question is: does God trust us in our finances?

The acronym D.E.B.T. can be an important tool in dealing with financial decisions in marriage. Without Discipline, Energy, a Budget and Trust we will all end up with DEBT. However, when couples receive the discipline of the Lord, focus their energy, prepare a budget, trust the Lord, debt-free living will be their reward.

My prayer for all married couples is: "Heavenly Father, you ordained marriage. Your word tells us when we are married we become one flesh. We must come together in our thinking and decision making. Lord, help all married couples to become united in their desire to seek your help in every area of life. We believe you want us to be free from debt. May married couples join together in their desire to be debt-free. In Jesus' name we pay. Amen."

NOTES:
How can your marriage use D.E.B.T.?

_____

_____

_____

_____

_____

_____

_____

_____

_____

_____

_____

_____

_____

_____

_____

_____

_____

_____

_____

_____

_____

_____

Avoid debt consolidation if it increases your total debt.

The rich rule over the poor and the borrower is servant to the lender.
~ Proverbs 22:7 (NIV)

CHAPTER 15

Borrowing

BASED ON MY fourteen years in banking, and fourteen years as a real estate developer the subject of borrowing has made a great impact on my life. Every week there are those who call me to inquire about how to borrow money or ask who they should talk to in obtaining a loan. Their requests are for a variety of issues related to borrowing.

Borrowing money is taken far too casually. Today, banks and other types of lending institutions spend millions of dollars trying to get and keep all of us in debt. We have all seen the credit card offer of "0%" for a year, with the opportunity to transfer all of our debt to the card. It is interesting to note the credit limit they give you on the new card is higher, so you can consolidate and get even deeper into debt as you continue to borrow from the new "cheaper." interest rate.

While it may be a good decision to consolidate higher interest rate accounts into a lower rate, we still must use caution to avoid getting deeper in debt. Proverbs 22:7 (NKJV) reads: *The rich rule over the poor and the borrower is servant to the lender.*

When faced with the financial decision of acquiring a loan, we need to focus on the most common types of questions. A word of caution—be sure to seek competent counsel in securing any type of financing. Let's look at some of the more common questions I get concerning obtaining a loan:

1. Is a loan consolidation good or bad?

a) Let me ask you this: Is the interest rate of the consolidation loan better than the individual loans? If so, it may be okay to consolidate. However, a consolidation loan must have a goal of getting us out of debt. Avoid a loan consolidation if it increases your total debt.

b) Are the payments on the consolidation loan for a longer period of time than on your existing loans? If so, use caution. Remember the goal is to get out of debt and not to just keep extending it.

c) Are you consolidating to get more money so you can spend more? If so, don't do it.

d) If you consolidate your loans, pay the largest payment you are able to make. This will pay the loan off faster (which should be your primary goal) and will reduce the amount of interest you pay.

e. By the way, unless you are operating on a budget and know how much you spend each month, you really don't know if a consolidation loan would be beneficial.

f. Avoid if possible, a consolidation loan if you are required to use your home as collateral. Protect your home equity. This issue has been addressed in a prior chapter.

2. Are low interest rates for a limited-time credit card offer a good deal? Yes, if you don't increase your credit limit or borrow more money. Be careful to see what happens when the limited time offer is over. What will the new interest rate be? Instead of getting a new card with a lower rate you may want to call your current credit card company and ask them if they will lower their rate. Tell them you are considering moving your balance to another card.

3. What does PITI mean on my mortgage statement/payment?

P – Principal

I – Interest

T – Taxes (on property)

I – Insurance

The total of these costs equals your monthly payment amount. If you paid less than 20% down on your mortgage, you may have something called PMI—Private Mortgage Insurance. This is an amount added to your PITI as an insurance premium you pay to insure the amount down you were not able to pay. After a few years, you may want to check on this. Once the value of your home increases you may be able to have the PMI removed from your total payment.

4. When obtaining a mortgage loan, be very careful that you understand the costs of your loan. Seek help in selecting you lender. Check with the Better Business Bureau or your states banking regulator before obtaining a loan.

Today, there are many types of mortgage lenders. Following is a list of a few:

a) Federal Housing Administration (FHA)

b) Veterans Administration (VA) Loans

c) See a realtor or attorney to help you understand the variations of FHA and VA loans.

d) Conventional loans have numerous options. Seek professional help. The down payment amount can be as little as 3% or as much as you can afford. Verify what additional costs will be charged to you over the interest rate. Be sure and request a good-faith estimate of your total costs. Be sure to seek professional help. Some pitfalls to look for in your documents are:

• A pre-payment penalty. This is a fee your lender may charge if you pay off your loan prior to the original maturity date.

• Be very careful to look for any balloon payments due prior to the loan maturity.

• When shopping for a loan, try to avoid prepaying points or fees unless the fees are for a credit report. Always seek professional or legal help. Some lenders offer 100% financing of the appraised value of the home, no cost loans, no job loans, no money down loans, investor purchase, owner occupant, or non-owner occupant loan, second home, previous bankruptcy, no income verification, and on and on. Because of the number of options regarding borrowing for homes today, you should always seek professional help.

5. No-cost loan: A true no-cost loan is a little hard to find. My experience has been that only one out of every twenty lenders will do a no-cost loan. A true no-cost loan is where your costs to obtain the loan are included in the interest rate you pay. The rate is higher, however you don't pay anything up front. In reality the loan costs are being paid by you.

6. How do I figure my mortgage payment amount? Seek competent professional help in obtaining any mortgage loan. Be sure to have them explain the PITI amounts.

7. What is an amortization schedule? This is a helpful tool in knowing how much of your monthly principal and interest payment is being applied to your actual principle balance. Ask your lender for an amortization schedule when you get your loan. Be sure to ask if you are allowed to make additional principle payments any time you desire to do so. By making additional principle payments you will be able to pay off your loan faster and save interest costs.

When signing loan documents, be sure to read them first. Recently, when I was borrowing money to buy a home, I called the bank and asked them to please send the loan papers to me a few days in advance of the loan closing date. The loan officer said in more than ten years of doing loans, no one had ever asked her to do this. She said nobody reads this stuff. Well, I received the loan package three days prior to closing and I took the time to carefully read the documents. There were several items I questioned, and I found more than $2,000 in charges I was able to get removed from my up-front costs.

I realize most people do not have the experience to understand all of their loan documents. However, it is in your best interest (pun intended) to seek help in understanding what you sign.

This is a good time to give an actual account of what might happen if you do not read what you sign. A dear friend of mine purchased a home without a real estate agent's help. He put 10% down on the purchase price and obtained a loan from an investor for the balance of the money needed.

Everything seemed great to him and his wife. After several years of living in this house and investing thousands of dollars in improvements, he received a letter in the mail from the mortgage lender. The letter simply read, "Per the terms of your mortgage note and deed of trust, we are requesting the payment of $25,000 plus interest to date to be paid in thirty days. This payment is in accordance with the documents you signed five years ago. Please remit within thirty days or else we will start foreclosure proceedings against the property."

My friend was shocked. He could not believe he owed $25,000 plus interest and he had only thirty days to come up with the money or else lose his home. He tried everything he could to get the money.

However, because of a loss of a job and medical problems, his credit was terrible. He was considering bankruptcy and now this. How could this happen? What went wrong? Was this an attack from the devil or was it just his fault.

With only days remaining before the foreclosure went into effect, he called me for help. I tried to help him but it was too late. He had signed something he had not read. He had made the error of not seeking help and, no it was not an attack by the devil. He had to accept the responsibility of his decision.

I wish I could tell you everything came out fine but I can't. This man lost his home and more than $50,000 of equity. What ever happened to him? Did he learn from his terrible experience? Several years later, he worked hard to reestablish his credit. He saved, paid off debt, and was ready to buy a home again. This time he hired a real estate agent. This time he knew he would do things right.

Unfortunately, because of his rush to obtain the mortgage loan, he could not get a loan from his local bank because of past credit problems. The mortgage companies declined his requests because the amount of his new loan payment would be more than his income could handle. He decided he would pray and ask God for help. He prayed and tried to get a loan. Decline after decline, he continued to press on to get a loan.

Let me suggest when we pray and ask God to help us obtain a car or home loan and we get decline after decline, maybe the answer God has for us is "no" or "not now." Well, my friend continued to push to get his house. He did get a loan and, yes, he did get into his new house.

However, you guessed it. About one year later after he signed the loan documents, he brought the loan to me to see if I would check out what the documents said about refinancing and having the interest rate reduced.

It took only about thirty minutes to see that the loan document was worse than the one he had signed several years ago on his first home. There were large principal payments due every three years and extremely high penalties for refinancing.

Unfortunately, he had returned to his prior mistakes and did not make the right choices. Within six months, he felt he was better off to let this house go back to the lender. It was more expensive than he could afford. Income he expected to come in did not materialize. He was banking on a future job promotion to pay for a current commitment. He realized his best loss would be to lose only the money he had invested and not invest more into a "money pit." He signed the home over to the investor (with legal help) and walked away.

Not to leave you discouraged for this man, he has since

recovered. Thank the Lord. He owns a beautiful home with a good clean loan. He is serving God at his church and is telling as many as he is able, his story of poor decisions, and trying to manipulate God to get what he wanted. He is helping others.

Borrowing is not always a bad thing. Many homes, hospitals and churches have been built through the proper use of a loan. The problems with borrowing usually come due to borrowing more then we can afford. The Bible explains the good and bad issues in borrowing. In a concordance look up the scriptures on lending, borrowing and guaranteeing loans.

One of the nicest things that can happen to us is to pay off a loan. When we pay off our mortgage loan we experience a freedom from debt that is wonderful and fulfilling.

My prayer for you is: "Lord, help us to start taking the necessary steps to be debt-free. We desire to have all of our debt paid off including our home. Lord, we know that borrowing can be something good and useful. Yet borrowing without knowledge can be destructive. May we learn from your instructions in Proverbs Chapter 3 concerning borrowing and debt. Help us to be open to seek help prior to signing any loan documents. Your word tells to seek wise counsel in every area of life. Holy Spirit help us not to be ashamed of asking questions about every type of borrowing. Our desire is to live debt-free. Help us Lord to achieve this desire. In Jesus' name I pray. Amen."

NOTES:
List what you have learned about borrowing.

_____

_____

_____

_____

_____

_____

_____

_____

_____

_____

_____

_____

_____

_____

_____

_____

_____

_____

_____

God is the one who gives you power
to be successful.

God is our source, and discipline
is the key to allowing Him to bless us.

The Lord will provide our financial
miracle when we submit to
His plan of discipline.

CHAPTER 16

Discipline

WEBSTER'S DICTIONARY DESCRIBES discipline as training, instruction, and correction. Discipline could be the single most important word to debt-free living. The word discipline is a misunderstood word. We think of judgment and or condemnation. Yet, when we read Hebrews 12:6 (NIV): *The Lord disciplines those He loves*, we see a different side of discipline. In this scripture we discover God disciplines because of His love for His people. The Lord disciplines us so we will be able to receive the fullness of His blessings.

The purpose of discipline in our finances is found in Hebrews 12:10 (NIV): *Our fathers disciplined us for a little while as they thought best; but God disciplines us for our good that we may share in His holiness. No discipline seems pleasant at the time, but painful. Later on, however, it produces a harvest of righteousness and peace for those who have been trained by it.*

Using the first letters in the word Discipline, I have listed ten areas I believe are the keys to unlocking the financial blessings of God in our life. Through these financial principles we can live debt-free:

Delight: We must have a desire to delight ourselves in the Lord. Psalm 37:4 (NKJV) reads: *Delight thyself also in the Lord and He shall give thee the desires of thine heart.*

If we desire a financial blessing, we must be delighted in serving God. We must never delight ourselves in money. If we desire to give more to the work of the Lord and live debt-free we must live our lives for Him. Without a desire to please God, our financial plan will never succeed. The Lord wants to bless us financially, yet we must have a desire to delight ourselves in Him and receive His discipline and direction.

Increase: This will be the result of discipline in our finances. Every time I meet with people to discuss their finances I bring up a word they dislike: Budgeting. Very few of those I meet have a budget or know how much it costs them to live from month to month. Most of them tell me they must be spending the amount they make each month.

As I mentioned in a previous chapter; my experience reveals that most individuals are spending $300 to $800 a month more than they make. That shortfall is covered with credit cards, more debt or savings withdrawals. The primary reason for over spending more than we make is a lack of discipline in our financial decisions and neglecting to set up a monthly budget of income and expenses. I believe a disciplined financial plan will open the gates for increase and debt-free living.

Source: If we believe God is our source for financial blessing, then we must turn to Him for discipline in our finances. We have already seen the Lord disciplines us for our own good. We must look to God as our source in all areas of our life. He is our source of financial and spiritual gain. Deuteronomy 8:19 (NKJV) says: *For it is He that giveth thee power to get wealth.* God is our source, and discipline is the key to allowing Him to bless us.

Choices are a major factor in our finances. Most people are limited in the amount of money they earn. However, all people are in control of the choices they make in spending. Since we were children, we have made choices on how we spend money. We choose to budget, we choose to tithe, we choose to control credit.

We choose to have discipline or we choose to ignore it. Let's choose discipline in our finances; discipline to budget, tithe, control spending, and make well planned purchases. When we do that it will take us into debt-free living. Let's all choose to be debt-free.

Deuteronomy 8:18 (NKJV): *And you shall remember the Lord your God, for it is He that gives you power to get wealth.*

The word of God is our instruction manual for every area of our life. When it comes to money the Lord has dedicated more than 1/6 of the Bible to help us know how He wants us to handle out finances.

Ephesians 6:4 (NASV) reads: *And fathers, do not provoke your children to anger; but bring them up in the discipline and instruction of the Lord.*

Every parent must discipline and instruct their children and when they do, it must be done with love for the child's benefit. Parents have the first, and can have the best, influence on how to make good choices.

Investment: We must invest our time and energy into the disciplines of this plan in order to live debt-free. When we decide to invest into a new way of thinking about the proper use of our income it will produce a great return to that investment. Are you investing enough time in evaluating your purchases?

Are you investing more time in how to make more money so you can spend more? If so, then how about investing more time in trying to spend less. Where your attention flows is where our money goes. We must invest in a plan that will return to us debt-free living.

Patience: A disciplined financial plan requires patience. I have discovered impulse buying (purchasing with little or no prior planning) is one of the single biggest challenges facing every family's financial plan. Retailers are trying to get us to impulse buy.

Just look at the checkout stand at all major discount stores. As you are waiting in line to check out, the stuff on the shelves are screaming out, "BUY ME, BUY ME." Your children are screaming out, "CAN I HAVE, CAN I HAVE?" Your credit card is saying, "USE ME, USE ME." We want to scream, but instead we give in to impulse buying. We lose patience, and ignore discipline. Let's decide to have patience with disciplined purchasing and not try the patience of God.

Lending: Have we ever thought about what it would be like to be out of debt and have such abundance that we could be a lender rather than a borrower? The word discipline may be the only thing holding us back from realizing that dream. Deuteronomy 15:6 (NASV) reads: *For the Lord your God shall bless you as He has promised you and you will lend too many nations but you will not borrow.* This scripture may seem a little bold for some. However, the blessing of our God is without limits.

Impossible: Most people I speak to feel they are in an impossible situation and nothing short of a miracle will turn their financial dilemma around. Jesus said in Luke 18:26 (NASV) *The things impossible with men, are possible with God.* The Lord will provide our financial "miracle" when we submit to His plan for discipline. Becoming debt-free may seem impossible to some. However nothing is impossible with our God.

Needs: When does a want become a need? When does a desire become a want that becomes a need? Many of those I meet have a difficult time understanding the difference between needs, wants and desires.

This is where you may get upset with me. However, we need to examine our costs to live in order to realize what must change in order to become debt-free. This may be a little painful but it can heal us financially.

Most of those I meet with will tell me they don't have enough income to cover their needs. Then we make a list of their monthly expenses.

Today I find it amazing to see how many people say they need four or five televisions in their home. In addition to that they need multiple cell phones. Their cable TV and internet costs can run $300 a month. Health club dues and hobbies can use up a lot of money. Some will have several large dogs or cats. In Arizona they may even have a couple of horses.

I told you this could be tough. Every one of us must decide what is a need, want or desire. When we clearly see how we deal with these three items we can start to realize what must change. The Lord promised to meet our need, not our greed.

Discipline must be the determining factor in establishing our needs. I believe we can have our wants and desires. However, we must prove faithful with little so we can be trusted with much. One of our needs is to be debt-free.

Entrusted: means to assign or commit. We have been entrusted to share our faith with others. The Lord has entrusted us with His promises. I believe the Lord is looking for those who are trustworthy with their finances. Those who accept the discipline of the Lord can be entrusted with true riches. Living a disciplined life proves to the Lord we will be trustworthy with little and with much. Jesus said in Luke 16:10 (NKJV): *He who is faithful in a very little thing is faithful also in much; and he who is unrighteous in a very little thing is unrighteous also in much. If therefore you have not been faithful in the use of unrighteous mammon (money), who will entrust the true riches to you?*

The statement: If only I made more money may be our worst enemy. That statement dominates the comments of those who have made questionable decisions in spending. Some believe more money is always the answer. Now that we have read these suggestions about how to live debt-free; we must decide what must change. We are the one who will be faced with making financial choices. It is up to us.

Now we are aware of what steps to take in order to get out of debt and stay debt-free. Most of the time it is not what we know but what we do with what we know that counts.

My prayer is from this day forward, we will seek God's Word for direction, accept his discipline, and make choices that are both Biblical and practically based.

In America, consumer debt is over one trillion dollars (not including mortgage loans). Bankruptcies in the year 2017 were nearly 800,000. Decide today not to become part of this statistic. Decide to experience freedom in your finances. Live your life debt-free.

My prayer for you is: "Lord, your word explains how important it is to live a disciplined financial life. Sometimes we struggle with being disciplined. Help us to be willing to accept your discipline. We receive this teaching because it will benefit my desire to live debt-free. In Jesus' name I pray. Amen."

NOTES:
List what must be changed.

_____

_____

_____

_____

_____

_____

_____

_____

_____

_____

_____

_____

_____

_____

_____

_____

_____

_____

_____

_____

In whom also we have obtained an inheritance.
~ Ephesians 1:11 (JKV)

A good person leaves an inheritance for their children's children.
~ Proverbs 13:22 (NIV)

CHAPTER 17

Our Inheritance

RECENTLY, WHILE I was preparing a Sunday message for our church, the word "inheritance" kept coming up in my reading and prayer time.

We all know what the word inheritance means: the acquisition of a possession; a transmission from parent to offspring; to receive as a right from an ancestor at his death. When we think of that word, we tend to believe we do not have any control over our inheritance. After all, someone has to die for us to be eligible.

Well, someone did give His life so we could receive our inheritance. His name is Jesus Christ, the Son of God, The Bright Morning Star, The Lamb of God, and The Messiah. Our inheritance is ours to claim. Ephesians 1:11(NKJ) reads: *In Him also we have obtained an inheritance, being predestined according to the purpose of Him who works all things according to the counsel of His will.*

How do we receive our inheritance? What can we do to claim the promises of God? We know every good and perfect gift comes from the Lord. In Jeremiah 29:11 we are told we have a future and a hope. Jesus tells us we can have life and have it more abundantly. Yet, how do I claim my inheritance?

The most obvious way to find our inheritance is by reading and studying the Word of God. Many read their Bibles on a daily basis. However, few study the Word of God. The only way we will discover the hidden promises of our inheritance is by studying the scriptures and asking the Holy Spirit to reveal truth.

One of my favorite passages is found in Jeremiah 33:3 (NKJV): *Call to me, and I will answer you, and show you great and mighty things, which you do not know.*

These words tell us our God desires to reveal His truths to us if we seek Him through His word. I promise you God's Word reveals the inheritance He has for us. Our inheritance is revealed from Genesis to Revelation. However, there are conditions to receive the Lord's inheritance He plans for us.

We may receive our earthly inheritance by keeping our eyes and ears open to the events taking place around us. When we listen to the radio, watch the news and sports on television, or read the newspaper we must be aware that our God is able to show us something that will bless us. Many times we rush through our day and miss reading, seeing, or hearing our earthly inheritance as the Lord places an idea or creative thought in our path.

A news article, advertisement, or want ad may be a piece of our earthly inheritance. In order to hear or see these hidden pieces of our earthly inheritance, we must seek help from the Holy Spirit. He is the one who sees and hears for us when we are running through life.

The Word of God tells us in Proverbs 13:22 (NKJ): *The wealth of the wicked are laid up for the righteous.*

Only by the Holy Spirit are we able to see our earthly inheritance. This would be a great time to ask the Holy Spirit to reveal your earthly inheritance to you, through the various forms of media, conversation, and what you see and hear every day.

Pray this right now: "Father, I know through the death and resurrection of your Son and my Savior the Lord Jesus Christ, I can claim my inheritance. Holy Spirit, I yield to your direction; open my eyes and ears to see and hear the inheritance on earth you have promised me. Reveal it to me in whatever way you desire. In Jesus' name I pray."

Don't just look to other Christians or your Pastor to find your earthly inheritance. Our God is not limited to revealing our inheritances only through our Christian friends. To receive our earthly inheritance of living debt-free, we must learn to live in Proverbs 3:5 (NKJV): *Trust in the Lord with all your heart and lean not on your own understanding.*

The word trust is spoken so easily but living in trust is something entirely different. Our earthly inheritance is discovered when we live to trust in our God. One way to know if we are living with trust in God is to ask the Holy Spirit to reveal to us what we should do in all financial decisions.

Let's take a look at trust in the area of giving offerings. Many times we listen to an evangelist or hear of a special need. We may think about giving $10.00 or $20.00. Let me suggest you test your trust in the Lord by praying and asking Him to reveal to you what you should give as an offering. Learn to trust Him. The Holy Spirit is not going to put you in bankruptcy by giving to His work. Yet, submitting to the Spirit is a giant step in opening up the windows of heaven to receive the Lord's promise of your inheritance.

I believe we have an earthly inheritance of living debt-free. Never forget that everything we inherit is a gift from God our father. He promised us an eternal inheritance when we accept His son Jesus as our Lord and Savior.

My prayer for you is: "Heavenly Father, I thank you for the inheritance you have promised us. When we become Christians we become heirs into the kingdom of God. In Jesus' name I pray. Amen."

NOTES:
List your desired earthly and spiritual inheritances.

_____

_____

_____

_____

_____

_____

_____

_____

_____

_____

_____

_____

_____

_____

_____

_____

_____

_____

_____

_____

_____

_____

_____

Happy is the man who finds wisdom, and the man who gains understanding.
~ Prov. 3:13 (NKJV)

Commit your works to the Lord, and your thoughts will be established,
~ Prov. 16:3 (NKJV)

CHAPTER 18

Plan For Retirement

WHEN YOUNG, WE seldom thought about retirement. The age of 65 seemed so very far away. After all, only old people needed to be concerned about an income at retirement. As I was working and saving, my financial focus was on increasing my net worth. Back then my ultimate goal was to be worth $1 million. I believed a $1 million net worth was all I would ever need. Sadly, I was mistaken and did not understand the importance of a guaranteed income after retirement. As a young man I set my retirement age at 50 to 55 years old. Little did I think of the possibility of living 30 to 35 years after I turned 55.

The other area I paid little attention to was the effect of inflation on my retirement. That is true for so many today who plan to retire. Most of those I talk to are not aware that a compounded 3% annual rate of inflation will cause their cost of living to more than double in less than twenty-five years. Look at an example of this. If you retire at 65 and believe your cost of living will be $50,000 a year it's difficult to imagine that at the age of 90 it may cost you $100,000 a year to pay for the same lifestyle you have today.

Although one million dollars is a considerable amount of money, it will not support a $50,000 a year lifestyle for 25 years because of the impact of inflation. Obviously, we expect to earn something on our $1,000,000. However, there will be times when it is difficult to earn anything and we may even see a loss of our principle. Today our concern should be about whether we will outlive our cash and other resources. Another way to say it is we must not run out of cash before we run out of living here on earth.

My comments are not intended to scare anyone. With proper planning almost everyone will be prepared to enjoy their retirement and never run out of money. It's sad to say but many of those who are 55 years old today will not be financially able to retire when they are 65 years old. This is a surprise to most of those who are nearing retirement.

Allow me to provide a few reasons why those approaching retirement are not prepared.

First, Americans stopped saving for a rainy day many years ago. As I went through my 20s, 30s and 40s I discovered the majority of my friends and acquaintances did not have savings to cover emergencies.

Secondly, instead of making a savings withdrawal to cover an emergency they were forced to use a credit card. When the credit card was introduced to Americans in the early 1970s it provided a security blanket for those who needed a way to pay for unexpected expenses. In addition it made them feel they could purchase their wants, needs and desires without needing to pay cash. Credit card use is a national crisis with many having over $15,000 in credit card debt. The credit card was being used as a purchasing tool to get what we want now with little concern about how to pay for it later.

Thirdly, a lack of discipline in spending has created generations of individuals who are not preparing for retirement.

Following is a chart that will demonstrate how a 3% annual inflation rate will impact our cost-of-living over 25 years. People say they will spend less when they retire. However, studies show most of us will spend a little more than we did when we worked. Travel and gifts to family, grandchildren and friends tend to increase during retirement. We have more time to do things and go to places where we spend more.

The following chart will be a new revelation to most of those who are facing retirement. Nearly everyone I speak to about retirement have not planned for inflation.

$60,000 Cost of living +3% annually compounded

Year 1: $60,000 – Year 10: $78,282

Year 2: $61,800 – Year 15: $90,748

Year 3: $63,654 – Year 20: $105,200

Year 4: $65,563 – Year 25: $121,954

Year 5: $67,529

Some might say using a 3% inflation rate is a little high. However, I would rather plan for a 3% rate and not be caught short of funds. If the inflation rate is less than my estimate you may have a cushion to cover your expenses.

It is shocking to see how inflation impacts our cost-of-living. History shows prices will double every twenty years. As we grow older we may spend less on food, travel. However medical expenses will most likely eat up those savings.

We all agree debt is a major problem for many today. For those who want to retire it can be devastating. The Bible tells us when we are in debt to someone we can become their servant. The burden of too much debt places us in bondage. As we grow older and approach retirement, debt will keep us from enjoying our dreams of traveling and spending time the way we desire.

The best way I know to keep out of debt is to know how much it costs us to live each month and to live within that amount. Our retirement will be impacted by many issues. Income, debt, inflation, and whether we are saving some of what we make each month will all impact our retirement. However nothing is more important than to understand our cost to live each month.

Over the past forty years, I have worked with thousands of individuals and couples to put together a correct list of personal expenses that make up their cost-of-living. My experience shows most spend more than they make annually. That overspending must be paid by savings withdrawals or increased debt.

As mentioned before, the credit card is the culprit for a large portion of overspending. Most debt is difficult to pay off and credit card debt is the worst.

Now let's put together a list of reoccurring and non-reoccurring monthly expenses. The non-recurring monthly costs are the ones that most do not include in their budget. Remember, a cost-of-living list or budget must include everything we spend money on every month over an entire year.

At the end of Chapter Five I have prepared a list of expenses to help in preparing your budget. Please take the time to prepare a realistic monthly budget.

A budget is the best tool to plan for retirement and to get out of debt. Some believe they are debt-free even though they have a home mortgage. Personally I don't have a problem with people going into retirement with a small home mortgage, provided they have the necessary retirement income to make that mortgage payment. Don't forget in most states our home will never be free from debt due to required property taxes. In addition everyone needs to pay for property insurance. Some will have homeowner's association fees.

I guess you could say our home is never really debt-free.

In retirement renting a home or apartment may be the best decision we will make. We can keep the cash from the sale of our home to invest and pay our expenses. Recently many of my friends have turned to renting instead of owning their home during retirement. I suggest you seek counsel from a good accountant, CPA or attorney in making this decision. Since I am not an investment advisor I will not make suggestions on how you should use the cash from the equity of your home if you decide to sell.

Retiring from our day job is something most work their entire life to attain. Retirement is different to all people. Some want to play golf, travel, garden or work on projects. To others retirement is fishing, reading, time with family and friends. Whatever your plans are don't let a lack of good financial planning today rob you of a great retirement. Most can and will retire debt-free if they start to plan for it today.

My prayer for you is: "May the Lord help all of us to prepare for retirement. We do not want to be dependent on our family for our financial needs after we retire. With your help Lord we will be able to adjust our spending. We will be debt-free before retirement. Thank you for your help Lord. In Jesus' name I pray. Amen."

NOTES:
List of things to get ready for retirement.

_____

_____

_____

_____

_____

_____

_____

_____

_____

_____

_____

_____

_____

_____

_____

_____

_____

_____

_____

_____

Most Frequently Asked Questions

1. How can I give more to the work of the Lord?

   Answer: Prepare a budget and live within it. Become a Tither. List below how and when you will do a budget.

   _____

   _____

   _____

   _____

   _____

   _____

   _____

   _____

   _____

2. Why do I run out of money each month?

   Answer: We run out of money before we run out of month because we do not know how much it costs to live each month. Estimate below how much you think you spend monthly. List your monthly income. After making this estimate, prepare an exact list of spending. Most of those I meet will spend far more than they make.

   _____

   _____

   _____

   _____

   _____

   _____

   _____

   _____

   _____

3. Is it okay to have wealth? Own an expensive car?

> **Answer:** Yes, as long as we put the work of the Lord first. Make a list of what you would do if you were wealthy. After making the list think of how much is for you personally and how much would be for helping others. Do you need to adjust your list?

_____

_____

_____

_____

_____

_____

_____

_____

_____

_____

4. How can I determine if my finances are improving each year?

> **Answer:** If your savings are growing and if your debt is decreasing.
>
> List what your debt was last year at this time? Now total up your debt today. Do the same with your savings. Are you pleased with the results?

_____

_____

_____

_____

_____

_____

_____

_____

_____

5. What is positive cash flow?

> **Answer:** To have more money coming in than is going out. Prepare a list of what you need to do to have positive cash flow. Focus more on reducing spending.

_____
_____
_____
_____
_____
_____
_____
_____
_____
_____
_____
_____
_____
_____

6. What is living below our means?

> **Answer:** Not spending everything we make. How do you feel about living below your income? Is spending more important to you than saving? Be honest with yourself.

_____
_____
_____
_____
_____
_____
_____
_____
_____
_____
_____
_____
_____

7. Why can't I keep money in my savings account?

> **Answer**: It is usually a lack of discipline and not having a budget. Is the word discipline difficult for you to deal with? Remember, the Lord disciplines those He loves. He knows discipline brings a blessing. List where you need discipline.

_____
_____
_____
_____
_____
_____
_____
_____
_____

8. Should I buy or lease a car? Should I buy or rent a home?

> **Answer**: For a car, it depends on how many miles you drive each year. For a home, it depends on how long you plan to live in it. Write down your plans for these two items. The Bible tells us we must plan our ways.

_____
_____
_____
_____
_____
_____
_____
_____
_____
_____
_____

9. Why should I budget? I know what I make.

> **Answer**: A budget organizes our spending. List why you need a budget.

_____

_____

_____

_____

_____

_____

_____

_____

_____

_____

_____

_____

10. All I need is a little more money, right?

> **Answer**: Usually it's not more money we need but a better understanding of how much we spend. Do you know the difference between needs, wants and desires? If you are married both you and your spouse must be in agreement on these issues. List them below and label them need, want or desire. This will be an interesting exercise.

_____

_____

_____

_____

_____

_____

_____

_____

11. Can I borrow money?

> **Answer**: There is nothing wrong with borrowing as long as we have a good plan to pay it off and get out of debt. Consolidating your debt will work only when we can control our spending. Avoid using your home equity to pay off loans. List what you believe needs to be consolidated.

---

12. In marriage, who should make the decisions?

> **Answer**: Both the husband and wife must jointly agree. Make a list of spending issues you are challenged with in your marriage. Ask the Lord to help you both come into agreement.

---

13. Can I co-sign and guarantee a loan for someone else?

>   **Answer**: No. It is better to borrow the money and have them pay you back. Never, loan money we can't afford to lose. List the times you have violated these instructions. This is not to make you feel bad. I suggest you do this so you will not make the same mistake again.

_____
_____
_____
_____
_____
_____
_____
_____
_____

14. Is it okay to have a credit card?

>   **Answer**: Yes, as long as we pay off the balance each month. Make a list of your credit cards and determine the best way to use them. If you have a difficult time controlling credit card use, please cut them up and cancel them.

_____
_____
_____
_____
_____
_____
_____
_____
_____
_____

15. Should I tithe on my gross or net income?

> **Answer**: Depends on whether we want to be blessed on our net or gross. If you are not tithing 10% of your gross income, make a list of what you need to do in order to tithe.

_____
_____
_____
_____
_____
_____
_____
_____
_____
_____
_____
_____

16. How can I improve my cost of living?

> **Answer**: Look for places to cut spending. Like cable, internet, cell phones etc. Car payments are a major issue. List what expenses you are able to reduce.

_____
_____
_____
_____
_____
_____
_____
_____
_____
_____
_____
_____

17. How long will it take to be debt-free?

> **Answer**: It depends on us. Most can be debt-free in ten years, including their mortgage. The length of time it will take to be debt-free is not as important as your commitment to prepare a plan and just do it. Write down when you will get started and what you must do.

_____
_____
_____
_____
_____
_____
_____
_____
_____
_____
_____

18. What is the best reason to give?

> **Answer**: The Holy Spirit puts it in our heart. Make a list of what you desire to give to. Beside each item explain why.

_____
_____
_____
_____
_____
_____
_____
_____
_____
_____
_____
_____
_____

19. How soon can I start to tithe once I have the desire?

> **Answer**: With a good budget and controlled spending most can start in 30-60 days. List what you need to do to start tithing.

_____

_____

_____

_____

_____

_____

_____

_____

_____

_____

_____

_____

20. Is it necessary to read every loan document?

> **Answer**: Yes, if you can't, then find someone you trust to read all documents. List any loan documents you have signed. Even though you may have signed loan documents without reading them, now is a good time to read them. You may find something you can prepare for.

_____

_____

_____

_____

_____

_____

_____

_____

_____

21. Is goal setting okay for a Christian?

> **Answer**: Yes. The Bile tells us to plan our ways. List your goals in all areas of your life. Financial goals are not the only area in which we need to establish goals.

_____
_____
_____
_____
_____
_____
_____
_____
_____
_____
_____
_____

22. Do budgets require lots of time?

> **Answer**: To get it started should take only a couple of hours. To keep it up will take only a few minutes each day. Then it will become a part of our life. Set a time and date to get started.

_____
_____
_____
_____
_____
_____
_____
_____
_____
_____
_____

23. How can I start a savings account?

> **Answer:** Just go to a bank and put in what you have to get it started. Take the first step and keep on stepping. Be careful the bank does not charge you a service fee when you have a small balance. Start with a small amount like $10 a week. Before long you will be able to increase your savings each week. List what you must do to start saving. Make a chart of how much you will have saved in only a few years. Add the amount of interest you will get from the bank and compound it every year. Ask the bank to do that for you when you open your account.

_____
_____
_____
_____
_____
_____

24. What are the steps to failure?

> **Answer:** Review Chapter Eight. After reading my example of steps to failure in chapter 8, make a list of financial mistakes you have made in the past on the lines below. Making a list of past errors will help you from making them again.

_____
_____
_____
_____
_____
_____

25. What are the steps to freedom?

> **Answer**: Review Chapter Eight. Once again, after you read the steps to financial freedom, make a list of the steps you need to take to be debt-free. Writing it down is always helpful.

_____

_____

_____

_____

_____

_____

_____

_____

_____

_____

_____

_____

_____

_____

26. Why is it true the more you make the more you spend?

> **Answer**: A lack of discipline. As I have mentioned previously, discipline is vital to becoming debt-free. List how you feel about always spending more when you make more.

_____

_____

_____

_____

_____

_____

_____

_____

_____

27. How do I make good decisions?

> **Answer**: Seek good advice. Read God's word. Write down the process you have in making financial decisions. If you do not have a defined process, then prepare one.

_____

_____

_____

_____

_____

_____

_____

_____

_____

_____

_____

_____

28. Is it possible to prosper financially and still serve God?

> **Answer**: A large number of wealthy individuals do. The Lord does not put a dollar amount on how much we can be worth financially. He does tell us to help meet the needs of others. How do you feel about this issue?

_____

_____

_____

_____

_____

_____

_____

_____

_____

_____

29. What causes Christians who get rich to turn from God?

> **Answer**: They have not prospered spiritually. Are you prepared to properly handle financial blessings? Write down how you would deal with getting rich.

---

30. How can I pay off my mortgage faster?

> **Answer**: Pay more on your principle each month above your regular payment. Write what steps you need to take to pay off your mortgage loan.

---

31. Why are so many filing bankruptcy today?

> **Answer**: They are operating in their own plan and not God's. List the ways to avoid filing bankruptcy.

_____

_____

_____

_____

_____

_____

_____

_____

_____

_____

_____

_____

32. Where is my best source of help to become debt-free?

> **Answer**: Start with payer. Then read God's word. Find someone who needs help in their finances and work with them. Write down the advice you would give to others to be debt-free.

_____

_____

_____

_____

_____

_____

_____

_____

_____

_____

_____

_____

My purpose in writing this book is to help you become debt-free. Believe in your heart it will happen to you. Apply the suggestions in this book and consistently adhere to them. Trust the Lord with your finances. When we do that we can expect to be blessed.

As I finish this writing my pray for you is: "Heavenly Father, may the lessons in these chapters become a part of our life. Help us Lord to live out the instructions you have given us in the book of Proverbs chapter 3. Because of the promises in your word we believe we are able to live debt-free.

"We believe your desire is to see your followers prosper and be in good health even as their soul prospers. Thank you Lord for all you have done and plan to do in our lives. We pray the Holy Spirit will help those who desire to enjoy debt-free living. In Jesus' name we pray. Amen."

FINAL NOTES:

_____

_____

_____

_____

_____

_____

_____

_____

_____

_____

_____

_____

_____

_____

_____

_____

_____

_____

_____

_____

_____

_____

FINAL NOTES:

ALSO BY DAVID C. FRIEND

Vietnam: Before-During-After: A Young Man's Journey

The Vietnam War created more division in America than all of America's modern day conflicts and wars combined. The culture of America was under attack. Free love, drugs, and anarchy were birthed in our country. With the assassinations of President John F Kennedy in 1963, Martin Luther King in 1968, Robert Kennedy in 1968 and the War in Vietnam, America was facing one of it's most turbulent times.

"My goal is to examine how young men and women were emotionally, spiritually and physically impacted by the Vietnam War. In this true story of a young man's journey, we see how the grace of God covered and protected a soldier who had not accepted Jesus as Lord. Eventually, through the witness of others, and a young man seeking more in life, we see God's plan for him come to fruition."

~ David C. Friend

PASTOR DAVID C. FRIEND – BIO

David Friend began his college education at Phoenix College. This was interrupted by his service in the military, including a year in Vietnam. Upon returning to the United States and completing his service, he graduated from Phoenix College.

He studied finance and lending at Western Bancor during his banking career. David was a part-time instructor in banking at seven community colleges in Arizona.

While working at First National Bank of Arizona and First Interstate Bank from 1969 to 1984, he served as Operations Officer, Branch Manager, Commercial Lender, Vice-President and Regional Manager and State Retail Sales Manager.

David was a Vice President and partner with a real estate development company for three years. He then owned and operated his own development firm, Dave Friend Homes, from 1987 to 1997.

In 1997, he went into full time ministry at Phoenix First Assembly. He was ordained by the Independent Assemblies of God in 1998 and started a new church called North Scottsdale Christian.

As Senior Pastor, the Lord blessed the church with over 1,000 members. In 2015, North Scottsdale Christian merged with Phoenix First Assembly, now Dream City Church.

Currently, David serves as a board member with Dream City Church. He is mentoring businessmen and speaks on finance and prayer.

David has served as a board member with Teen Challenge, Grand Canyon University Foundation, Paradise Valley Chamber of Commerce, Tucson Salvation Army, several churches and non-profit organizations.

He resides in Scottsdale Arizona with his wife, Sharon. They have two married children and six grandchildren.

.